Atmabodha

आत्मबोध

by
Ādi Śaṅkarācārya

Commentary by
Swami Chinmayananda

Central Chinmaya Mission Trust

Printed from Oct 2004 to Aug 2009 - 32,200 copies
Second Edition - May 2011 - 3,000 copies
Third Edition - December 2012 to June 2023 - 21,200 copies
Reprint - April 2025 - 3,,000 copies

Published by:
Chinmaya Prakashan
The Publications Division of
Central Chinmaya Mission Trust
Sandeepany Sadhanalaya,
Saki Vihar Road, Powai, Mumbai - 400 072, India.
Tel.: +91-22-2803 4900
Email: ccmtpublications@chinmayamission.com
Website: www.chinmayamission.com

Distribution Centre in the USA:
Chinmaya Publications West
560 Bridgetown Pike
Feasterville, PA 19053-7240, USA
Tel.: (215) 396-0390, Fax: (215) 396-9710
Email: publications@chinmayamission.org
Website: www.chinmayapublications.com

Designed by: Chinmaya Kalpanam, Mumbai.

Printed by: SAP Print Solutions Pvt. Ltd., Mumbai

ISBN: 978-81-7597-512-5

Preface

CCMT is delighted to present before its readers the revised edition of *Ātmabodha* with a revamped cover and layout, thus meeting a longstanding demand. We have also attempted to eliminate all errors and have incorporated diacriticals making the book as reader-friendly as possible.

Ātmabodha is an introductory text to Vedānta. Ādi Śaṅkarācārya as a poet has succeeded in painting the ideals of Vedānta not only with beautiful examples and similes but also with logical explanations.

Pūjya Gurudev Swami Chinmayananda takes us on a journey of spiritual wisdom by expounding this text in modern day terms and for the common man's understanding.

We thank Chinmaya Prakashanam and Chinmaya Kalpanam team for the efforts they have taken to bring out this beautiful book.

We are positive that the readers will benefit from reading and reflecting upon the wise words of the Masters.

Central Chinmaya Mission Trust
Mumbai - 400 072

Transliteration and Pronunciation Guide

In this book, Devanagari characters are transliterated according to the scheme adopted by the International Congress of Orientalists at Athens in 1912. In it one fixed pronunciation value is given to each letter; f, q, w, x and z are not called to use. According to this scheme:

Devanagari	Translit-eration	Sounds Like	Devanagari	Translit-eration	Sounds Like
अ	a	son	ढ्	ḍh	adhesive*
आ	ā	father	ण्	ṇ	under*
इ	i	different	त्	t	tabla
ई	ī	feel	थ्	th	thumb
उ	u	full	द्	d	this
ऊ	ū	boot	ध्	dh	Gandhi
ऋ	ṛ	rhythm*	न्	n	nose
ॠ	ṝ	**	प्	p	pen
ऌ	ḷ	**	फ्	ph	phantom*
ए	e	evade	ब्	b	boil
ऐ	ai	delight	भ्	bh	abhor
ओ	o	core	म्	m	mind
औ	au	now	य्	y	yes
क्	k	calm	र्	r	right
ख्	kh	khan	ल्	l	love
ग्	g	gate	व्	v	very
घ्	gh	ghost	श्	ś	shut
ङ्	ṅ	ankle*	ष्	ṣ	sugar
च्	c	chuckle	स्	s	simple
छ्	ch	witch*	ह्	h	happy
ज्	j	justice	ं	ṁ	improvise
झ्	jh	Jhansi	ः	ḥ	**
ञ्	ñ	banyan	क्ष्	kṣ	action
ट्	ṭ	tank	त्र्	tr	three*
ठ्	ṭh	**	ज्ञ्	jñ	gnosis
ड्	ḍ	dog	ऽ	’	a silent ‘a’

* These letters don’t have an exact English equivalent. An approximation is given here.
** These sounds cannot be approximated in English words.

Introduction

No scientific textbook can be prescribed to the students without an initial chapter giving the definition of the terms and terminologies that are used in the body of the book. The scientist visualises the world from his viewpoint, he sees those facts and truths which are not visible to others. Since he sees visions which are not the common property of all, in his language he will have to use unconventional words which have for him some special imports and secret suggestions. If these extraordinary words are not rightly understood by the teacher and the taught, transfer of knowledge would be impossible. Therefore, in every textbook of science, the first few chapters describe the categories.

Sufferings and sorrows form a part of life's games. There is none who has not undergone pressing agonies in his own day-to-day life, either physically, mentally or emotionally. Yet, nobody seems to invite them. In fact whatever we do is to avoid, as far as possible, this aspect of life coming in contact with us. The more we want to escape its cruel jaws, the more it takes an endless variety of subtler and sharper ways of attacking.

Physical ailments form but one tribe of hordes that barbarously attack us; even more relentless and cruel are our mental sufferings. As we progress in our knowledge of the curative processes for ameliorating the physical sufferings, we observe that the mind's ill health affects the body much more than what one could imagine; and this kind of suffering proves all the more difficult to deal with. Mental disintegration is more dangerous, for it brings about not only misery to the sufferer but also a kind of dangerous disharmony in and excruciating intolerance with the surroundings of such an individual.

On the whole, it means that each one of us who is suffering (and is there anyone who is not?) from this inner malady is an unhappy centre, spreading unhappiness and restlessness all around oneself. A solution to these problems, very complicated and extremely confusing to the average mind, is what we seek individually and collectively. The results of such investigations conducted by the ancient ṛṣis and the data collected from their personal experiences constitute the bulk of our scriptures.

Today, instead of searching for any radical solution and specific cure for this problematic disease and consequent suffering in life, what man actually does in society is to collect around him various kinds of escape distractions and compromise dopes, through all kinds of foul methods. He vainly hopes to drown his sorrows in ever so many unhealthy indulgences. By these methods, at best man succeeds in turning his mind away from the actual facts of life as they are. To analyse scientifically and to observe closely, the nature and behaviour of our outer world of objects and the inner instruments of experience in us are the methods employed in the Upaniṣads, by which the seers have discovered a happy solution for the great problems of man and his life.

Vedānta is the science of life. It explains the art of living. It points out the ultimate goal of existence and provides schemes and methods by which sincere seekers can easily make their pilgrimage successful. Since the Teacher has to point out a goal transcending the ordinary realms of experiences, he has to borrow his vocabulary from the everyday language and present them, no doubt, strangely dressed up in special significances. Naturally, the obvious dictionary meaning will not be a true guide in digesting and assimilating the declarations of the scriptures.

The golden key, by which the scriptures are opened and its divine Knowledge brought out, is found in the books like *Ātmabodha,* which explains exhaustively the categories in Vedānta. Such volumes are known as the prakaraṇa granthas.

Knowledge available in the world of books is found in two types of records – textbooks of the science explaining the theory and technique are known as the śāstras and the books that explain the terms and terminologies used in the śāstras are known as the prakaraṇa granthas. *Pañcadaśī, Vivekacūḍāmaṇi, Tattvabodha, Ātmabodha* are some of the examples of the latter type of books. They explain the śāstras but they do not contribute any original thought.

Śrī Śaṅkara took upon himself as his life's great mission, the reorientation of Hinduism. After having written his commentaries upon the sacred books of our culture, he provided the seekers with a voluminous devotional literature, singing his own love of the Lord. In the days of his perfect maturity, he took up his pen to write 'introductory books', introducing the theme of Vedānta for the infants in the spiritual world. *Ātmabodha* is one of them. This is not an original book inasmuch as there is not a single idea in it which is an entirely original contribution of Śrī Śaṅkara. Everyone of them is culled from the garden of the Upaniṣads and strung together on the chord of his poetry, interspersed with his exquisite simile. This wonderful garland so offered by Śaṅkara to adorn Mother Śṛuti is *Ātmabodha*.

As a modern materialistic man comes to study more and more the contents of the Upaniṣads, it is possible that he feels cheated of the cheaper joys of his previous easier life of mental distraction and physical dissipations. This negative feeling of a nameless sad regret saps all enthusiasm in the student. But this feeling comes only so long as one has not fully realised the fact that the enchanting fascinations of usual broadway distractions have a knack of wearing away too soon; one gets quickly bored of such superficialities.

An intelligent person very quickly loses all his attractions for such things. He discovers that his mind has a tendency to fly away from all its objects of entertainment and come to torment itself by its own thoughts that are indeed very unpleasant. A man of indiscriminate intellect never questions why it is so but instead he hurriedly discovers a new set of excitements and a fresh pattern of distractions to engage his mind's momentary fancy. He may even turn to God of the usual formalist religions - visit churches, mosques or temples, give away something in charity, build a house of God or a hospital, run to a hall of sermons and even take up to some forms of prayer. All of them are again, a new variety of distractions to keep his mind away from weeping at itself and thus escape its own suicidal brutalities.

People, who thus follow religion as an escape from themselves, ultimately come to gain nothing except perhaps a lingering sorrow dulled by a blind faith that benumbs the very capacity to perceive their own tragedies of life. Scientific detachment, honest observation, logical conclusions and heroic decisions alone can help an individual to come away from his own life's fallacies. *Ātmabodha* supplies all these requisites and Ācārya Śaṅkara has made this scientific treatise a chiselled beauty with a distinct cadence and rhythm of its own.

The poet in Śaṅkara revels in these sixty-eight verses. There is no verse here which does not have a simile. Each is a picture, a sure and striking example. These examples are real hammer strokes that nail the elusive ideals of Vedānta on to the immature comprehension of all early students.

They are all such striking examples, so pregnant with suggestions that to ruminate upon them is in itself a profitable meditation for the new initiates.

May the infinite Effulgence, the silent witness of all our actions, bless us all.

Meditation

ॐ

प्रातः स्मरामि हृदि संस्फुरदात्मतत्त्वं
सच्चित्सुखं परमहंसगतिं तुरीयम्।
यत् स्वप्नजागरसुषुप्तमवैति नित्यं
तद्ब्रह्म निष्कलमहं न च भूतसङ्घः॥

prātaḥ smarāmi hṛdi saṁsphuradātmatattvaṁ
saccitsukhaṁ paramahaṁsagatiṁ turīyam,
yat svapna-jāgarasuṣuptamavaiti nityaṁ
tad-brahma niṣkalamahaṁ na ca bhūtasaṅghaḥ.

In the early hours of the day I meditate upon the essential Self clearly experienceable in the heart-cave – that which is Existence-Knowledge-Bliss in nature – that which is the supreme goal, the Paramahaṁsa state – that which is the fourth plane of consciousness – which constantly illumines all experiences in the dream, waking and deep sleep conditions – I am that partless Brahman – Not (this) assemblage of matter envelopments.

Ātmabodha

Verse 1

तपोभिः क्षीणपापानां शान्तानां वीतरागिणाम्।
मुमुक्षूणामपेक्ष्योऽयमात्मबोधो विधीयते ॥ १ ॥

tapobhiḥ kṣīṇapāpānāṁ śāntānāṁ vītarāgiṇām,
mumukṣūṇāmapekṣyo'yamātmabodho vidhīyate. (1)

तपोभिः – by austerities; क्षीणपापानां – for those who have purified themselves; शान्तानाम् – for those who are peaceful; वीतरागिणाम् – for those who are free from cravings; मुमुक्षूणाम् – for those who are desirous of Liberation; अपेक्ष्यः – hoping for, expecting to gain; अयम् – this; आत्मबोधः – the knowledge of the Self; विधीयते – is composed

1. *I am composing this Ātmabodha, the treatise on the Self-knowledge, for those who have purified themselves by austerities, who are peaceful in heart, who are free from cravings and are desirous of Liberation.*

As a preamble, the great Teacher, Ādi Śaṅkara, himself a person of Self-realisation, lays down certain qualifications for those who wish to take up the study of this text. The verse also indicates the four aspects of the theme discussed, technically known as the 'anubandha catuṣṭayam'.

Such an introduction is justified, when we recognise that Śrī Śaṅkara was prescribing here an easy textbook. As he himself was a true educationist, he knew the type of students he had in his mind to whom he wanted to deliver the lessons. A high sounding style, erudite discussions, elaborate argumentations and so on, would be useless in serving the ordinary students who have discovered in themselves a growing enthusiasm to understand a little of the philosophy of Vedānta.

In this verse the term 'Ātmabodha' suggests the subject dealt with and the word 'mumukṣu' (one with a burning aspiration for Liberation) suggests that the object aimed at is the emancipation of the individual fromall his sense of bondage. The four qualifications necessary for an individual to be fit for the study of this text are – (a) discrimination of the Real and the unreal; (b) detachment from the unreal; (c) the sixfold wealth of goodness such as calmness and so on, and (d) the compelling desire for Self rediscovery.

One can claim to have read volumes of books and exhausted a whole library of the printed matter from its shelves; yet, he may still be useless in the practical application of his knowledge. In the study of philosophy mere book knowledge will be ineffective when the man of study enters the field of activities. Every earnest seeker must digest the knowledge gained until it grows into convictions, which can then be translated into actions.

When a book is written by a teacher, it is always intended for a certain type of student he has in his mind.

Every textbook is addressed to a certain class of students having some given qualities. They alone will be the most benefited by that given textbook. In the opening verse of the *Ātmabodha,* Ācārya Śaṅkara is trying to explain the type of audience to whom he is addressing in this tiny book.

Every attempt at living in self-control in all our contacts with the outer world, wherein all the efforts are dedicated for the higher purpose of evolving ourselves into a diviner being is known as 'tapas'. From pilgrimage and fasting to japa and dhyāna, all spiritual endeavours at self-control are different types of tapas. Through these methods one's sins (pāpas) become weaker.

Sin is not an action in itself but it is the tendency (vāsanā) to live and think negatively, which is left over in our mind as the result of our own wrong actions. These sinful tendencies become weak, when we practise self-control over a period of time.

When we have thus quietened our physical agitations through conscious and divinely dedicated self-control (tapas), the natural result is a growing sense of calmness in the heart. And when the mind has thus calmed down, the rate of fluctuations created by desires and attachment will also get reduced to a minimum.

An individual who has thus – (a) weakened his wrong tendencies through tapas, (b) who has consequently found in himself a relatively greater mental quietude, (c) in whom the desire agitations are temporarily at rest, (d) who is a sincere seeker wanting to liberate himself from personality shackles known and experienced within – he is the one who is fit for the study of *Ātmabodha*.

This does not disqualify anyone from reading and studying the text but only suggests various inner adjustments by which a student can make himself better tuned up to the contents of this book and come to understand better the theme discussed in it.

Verse 2

बोधोऽन्यसाधनेभ्यो हि साक्षान्मोक्षैकसाधनम् ।
पाकस्य वह्निवज्ज्ञानं विना मोक्षो न सिध्यति ॥ २ ॥

bodho'nyasādhanebhyo hi sākṣānmokṣaikasādhanam,
pākasya vahnivajjñānaṁ vinā mokṣo na sidhyati. (2)

बोधः – Knowledge; अन्यसाधनेभ्यः – in comparison with other means; हि – indeed; साक्षात् – direct; मोक्षैकसाधनम् – the only means for Liberation; पाकस्य – for cooking; वह्निवत् – just as the fire; ज्ञानं – knowledge; विना – without; मोक्षः – Liberation; न – not; सिध्यति – is accomplished

2. *Just as the fire is the direct cause for cooking, Knowledge is the direct means of Liberation. Compared to all other forms of discipline, knowledge of the Self is the only direct means of Liberation.*

In the previous verse having stated so much about the need for the practice of austerity, self-control and so on, one may misunderstand that discipline alone may lead one to the divine goal. To remove that misunderstanding, it is stated that Knowledge alone is the only direct means for Liberation.

The example given here and in almost everyone of the subsequent verses is to illustrate the case in point as clearly as possible to the new entrant in the field of Vedānta. In cooking food, items such as vegetables, rice, spices and so on, are contributory causes but by themselves they can never constitute food. Fire alone can accomplish the cooking; fire is the direct means. Similarly, the performance of rituals, offering of gifts, practice of austerities, control of the mind, the study of scriptures, the power of discrimination, are all no doubt helpful factors which aid one's spiritual growth but they do not by themselves directly lead one to Liberation. Liberation is possible only when the knowledge of the Self is gained and the glory of our true Self is rediscovered. This point is elaborated in the next verse.

Verse 3

अविरोधितया कर्म नाविद्यां विनिवर्तयेत्।
विद्याविद्यां निहन्त्येव तेजस्तिमिरसङ्घवत्॥ ३॥

avirodhitayā karma nāvidyāṁ vinivartayet,
vidyāvidyāṁ nihantyeva tejastimirasaṅghavat. (3)

अविरोधितया – since it is not opposed to; कर्म – action; न – not; अविद्यां – ignorance; विनिवर्तयेत् – destroys; विद्या – Knowledge; अविद्यां – ignorance; निहन्ति – destroys; एव – verily; तेजः – light; तिमिरसङ्घवत् – as deep darkness

3. *Action cannot destroy ignorance, as it is not opposed to ignorance. Knowledge does verily destroy ignorance just as light destroys deep darkness.*

Why is it not possible for the austerities and discipline to give what Knowledge can offer us? In this verse, the word 'Knowledge' is used in a figurative sense. The attainment of Knowledge really means the rediscovery of the Self in us which has never been non-existent. It is like the dreamer gaining the knowledge of the waker, then alone can the dreamer's dream-sorrow end. If the Ātman be, as described in the scriptures, ever-present, all-pervasive, complete and so on, then It is not to be striven for and obtained from somewhere, because It is already within us. Therefore, even divine actions do not, in the sense of a direct cause and effect, lead to the knowledge of the Self. It only helps in cleansing the inner equipments to perfection, the mirror in which we can see the true and the real nature of our own Self.

Supposing there is darkness in a room, sweep it for hours or let an army of men carry the darkness in baskets and pour it out, the room will still be in darkness! Sweeping is not the right method of removing darkness. Now, let us take some kind of light in our hand and enter the dark chamber. However thick the darkness be, in a moment, it will be illumined. Similarly, the ignorance (ajñāna) in us that envelops the pure light of Self-knowledge has seemingly veiled It. The luminous Consciousness, the Self, is ever bright and the enveloping ignorance has only to be brushed aside. Remove the misunderstanding about your true nature and the Ātman stands revealed. One need not discover It somewhere but one has only to remove the veil of ajñāna and It is rediscovered. In this sense alone it is stated that action cannot destroy ignorance. Knowledge alone is the antidote for ignorance.

Verse 4

परिच्छिन्न इवाज्ञानात्तन्नाशे सति केवलः।
स्वयं प्रकाशते ह्यात्मा मेघापायेंऽशुमानिव ॥ ४ ॥

paricchinna ivājñānāttannāśe sati kevalaḥ,
svayaṁ prakāśate hyātmā meghāpāyeṁ'śumāniva. (4)

परिच्छिन्नः – finite; इव – as if; अज्ञानात् – because of ignorance; तत् – that; नाशे सति – when destroyed; केवलः – alone; स्वयं – by Itself; प्रकाशते – reveals; हि – verily; आत्मा – the Self; मेघापाये – when clouds pass away; अंशुमान् – the sun; इव – like

4. *The Self appears to be finite because of ignorance. When ignorance is destroyed, It is recognised to be infinite, absolute. The Self reveals Itself by Itself – like the sun when the clouds pass away.*

The same main idea contained in the last verse is elaborated here. When it is stated that Knowledge alone destroys ignorance, it means, mere ritualistic actions cannot bring about the desired result. We need not make the sun shine by any means whatsoever. It is ever bright, high up in the sky, by itself illumining the world all the seasons round. It is the passing clouds that hide the vision and glory of this life-giving luminary, the sun. As the clouds pass away, the sun gets revealed.

The Self is infinite. There is in fact no multiplicity or plurality in that one homogenous Being, the wielder of all destiny. But it is because of our misunderstanding and the consequent superimpositions that we come to labour under the ignorance about this supreme Being. The Self alone exists as the illuminator, and makes Its presence known by Its life-giving power. Truly, therefore, this Ātman in Its supreme glory is unparalled in Its existence and reveals Its own 'Sat-Cit' nature, by Itself. Those who are qualified to experience this Truth are ones who have no clinging attachment to the enchanting objects of the world outside.

Verse 5

अज्ञानकलुषं जीवं ज्ञानाभ्यासाद्विनिर्मलम् ।
कृत्वा ज्ञानं स्वयं नश्येज्जलं कतकरेणुवत् ॥ ५ ॥

ajñānakaluṣaṁ jīvaṁ jñānābhyāsādvinirmalam,
kṛtvā jñānaṁ svayaṁ naśyejjalaṁ katakareṇuvat. (5)

अज्ञानकलुषं – defiled by ignorance; जीवं – the egocentric self; ज्ञानाभ्यासात् – by constant practice of Self-knowledge; विनिर्मलम् – pure; कृत्वा – having made; ज्ञानं – Self-knowledge; स्वयं – itself; नश्येत् – disappears; जलं – water; कतकरेणुवत् – as the powder of the 'kataka-nut'

5. *Constant practice of Self-knowledge purifies the egocentric self which is defiled by ignorance and having bestowed Self-knowledge, it itself disappears, just as the powder of the 'kataka-nut' settles down after it has cleaned the muddy water.*

In this verse an individual is defined as the Self that has been defiled by ignorance. Spiritual ignorance gives rise to the agitations of the intellect and the blabbering of the mind. The mind-intellect equipment reflects the light of the Consciousness, and the Self thus conditioned by the mind and intellect is the individual (jīva). The one suffering the limitations of matter is this ego which is comparable with our own reflections that we see in mirrors. It is but natural that we look distorted if the reflecting surfaces are concave or convex.

The ugliness of our reflections can end only when the reflecting surfaces are either destroyed or straightened. Similarly, the perversions of the individual can be ended only when the mind-intellect equipment has become steady and clean. An absolutely clean and steadied mind is no more a mind, since mind is but a thought flow. Where the mind has ended, there the egocentre perceived so long, existing as the sense of individuality, rebounds to its original nature, the Self.

The quietude of the mind and the ultimate sublimation of all its thought currents is a single process accomplished by meditation – jñānābhyāsa. The process of negating our identifications with the false matter envelopments and asserting our divine spiritual nature, constitutes the art of meditation and this process is explained exhaustively in the verses that follow in this very textbook.

If the continuous memory of 'I am the matter' is the egocentre, no doubt, it can be replaced by another constant thought current as 'I am the Self'. However, even that is a continuous thought flow and, therefore, even that experience (vṛtti-jñānam) is only a conditioned and finite one which cannot be Absolute.

This doubt is answered in the verse under discussion, where it is said that meditation after having sublimated the mind ends itself. Our attempts to sleep end when we start sleeping. The example given here is that of the clearing-nut plant (kataka), the powder of which was used in ancient India for cleaning muddy water. During the rainy season, when the wells or river water were all muddy, they used to put the powder of the kataka-nut plant on the surface of the water in their buckets. The powder becomes slightly slimy and forms a continuous film. Being denser, it settles down carrying along with it all minute particles of dirt, held suspended in the water. In the process not only the dirt goes down but the agent we had used also settles down leaving the clear water in the bucket, which can be decanted and used. In modern times, we use a little alum which also acts much the same way.

Verse 6

संसारः स्वप्नतुल्यो हि रागद्वेषादिसङ्कुलः ।
स्वकाले सत्यवद्भाति प्रबोधे सत्यसद्भवेत् ॥ ६ ॥

saṁsāraḥ svapnatulyo hi rāgadveṣādisaṅkulaḥ,
svakāle satyavadbhāti prabodhe satyasadbhavet. (6)

संसारः – the world; स्वप्नतुल्यः – like a dream; हि – verily; रागद्वेषादिसङ्कुलः – full of attachments, aversions and so on; स्वकाले – in its duration; सत्यवत् भाति – appears to be real; प्रबोधे सति – when awake; असत् – unreal; भवेत् – becomes

6. *The world which is full of attachments, aversions and so on, is like a dream. It appears to be real as long as the dream continues but becomes unreal when one wakes up – when true wisdom dawns.*

It is a common knowledge that in a dream the mind creates for itself a fanciful existence. Unfulfilled desires, passions and emotions, which we carry in our minds when we go to bed, often manifest in our dreams. That is why, he who has a balanced and controlled mind, who is not tossed by anger, pride and petty jealousies, likes and dislikes, does not wander away into wild dreams created by his feeble mind. It is the weak person who is a victim of his unfulfilled desires and thoughts.

In the dreamworld we have a variety of experiences[1]. In the waking state also experiences exist but we are not prepared to accept the waking state as a prolonged dream. The reason is the firm grip of 'avidyā' which prevents us from accepting the Real. We have not fully qualified ourselves to understand and realise the ephemeral nature of the existence of the objects around us and of our own exact relationship with our body, mind and intellect.

The dream is quite real to us so long as we are in it. Once we wake up, we realise the falsity of the entire experience. Similarly, when we go deep into the layers of the matter envelopments and experience the all-pervading Consciousness, the pluralistic existence rolls off; we are awakened to that supreme Self and thereafter the Self alone is experienced as Real. Therefore, wake up from the unreal existence by tearing asunder the ignorance (avidyā) that is covering the real Knowledge and realise the blissful nature of your own Self.

---

[1] For a more detailed and exhaustive treatment of this dream analogy read Swamijī's discourses on *Māṇḍūkya-upaniṣad with Kārikā.*

Verse 7

तावत्सत्यं जगद्भाति शुक्तिकारजतं यथा ।
यावन्न ज्ञायते ब्रह्म सर्वाधिष्ठानमद्वयम् ॥ ७ ॥

tāvatsatyaṁ jagadbhāti śuktikārajataṁ yathā,
yāvanna jñāyate brahma sarvādhiṣṭhānamadvayam. (7)

तावत् – so long as; सत्यं – real; जगत् – world; भाति – appears; शुक्तिकारजतं – silver in the mother-of-pearl; यथा – like; यावत् – as long as; न – not; ज्ञायते – is realised; ब्रह्म – Brahman; सर्वाधिष्ठानम् – the substratum for all; अद्वयम् – one without a second

7. *The world appears to be real, so long as Brahman, the non-dual substratum of the entire creation, is not realised. It is like the illusion of silver in the mother-of-pearl.*

'Jagat' is not to be understood only as the gross outer world, as we usually conceive it to be. It is the total experience of an individual in the three states of existence – the waking, dream and deep sleep states – experienced through the different types of equipments – physical, mental and intellectual. In short, jagat includes the world of objects cognised for enjoyment as forms, tastes and so on, through the sense organs; as feelings and emotions experienced by the mind; and as ideas and ideologies lived by the intellect. The sum total of all experiences gained through our gross, subtle and causal bodies is jagat.

As long as one has not entered into the divine state of God-consciousness through the realisation of the one absolute Truth, which is the substratum for all (sarvādhiṣṭhāna) and which pervades all manifestations, so long does the jagat appear to be very true and fully real. As long as we are in the dream state, we cannot believe that the dream we are experiencing is unreal. But when we wake up from the dream, we do not mourn for what we might have gained therein. Also, just as on waking up all the variety experienced in the dream state vanishes to become one with the waking mind, so too, on our spiritual awakening, all the plurality of this multiple world and all our different experiences will merge into that one supreme essence, the substratum for everything.

When we have realised this supreme Truth and begun to experience the presence of the eternal God Principle, the infinite Reality, the highest plane of pure Consciousness, which runs in and through us and everywhere, we no more mistake the jagat as real or as existing apart from that Conscionsness; just as we no more mistake the mother-of-pearl to be a silver piece once we have recognised its worthless calcium content.

In the illusion of a snake on a rope, without the rope – the substratum – the superimposition of the snake is impossible. Likewise, without the supreme Self, which is immortal, imperceptible and changeless, which is referred to as the substratum (adhiṣṭhāna), even the delusion as jagat is not possible.

Verse 8

उपादानेऽखिलाधारे जगन्ति परमेश्वरे ।
सर्गस्थितिलयान्यान्ति बुद्बुदानीव वारिणि ॥ ८ ॥

upādāne'khilādhāre jaganti parameśvare,
sargasthitilayānyānti budbudānīva vāriṇi. (8)

उपादाने – which is the material cause; अखिलाधारे – which is the support of everything; जगन्ति – the worlds; परमेश्वरे – in the supreme Self; सर्गस्थितिलयान् यान्ति – rise, exist and dissolve at the end; बुद्बुदानि – bubbles; इव – like; वारिणि – in the water

8. *Like bubbles in the water, the worlds rise, exist and dissolve in the supreme Self, which is the material cause and the support of everything.*

As compared to the thinkers of other religions, the Hindu thinkers of the past seem to have given greater attention to the principle of creation. This acute analytical approach to problems of life can, in its thoroughness and completeness, beat even many of the modern scientific methods.

Nothing new is ever created by anyone. The entire creation is nothing but change of forms, names, nature and conditions. Reconversion alone is creation. In thus creating a thing, three essential factors are necessary and together they are known as the cause.

In any creation three types of causes must come into play – the material cause, the efficient cause and the instrumental cause. In the case of a potter making a pot on his wheel with clay, the potter is the efficient cause, the wheel is the instrumental cause and the clay is the material cause (upādāna kāraṇa). In all pot creations in the world, the potter is separate from the clay; however in the creative process of the finite emerging from the Infinite, the material cause and efficient cause are one and the same. Just as bubbles in the water are but water rising in water, existing in water and when they burst, merging back to become water, so too is the plurality, cognised by the body, mind and intellect, all a play of names and forms upon the infinite Consciousness, the eternal divine substratum.

However, the supreme Brahman undergoes no change; being Absolute, It can suffer no modification in Itself. In that case, how can the world of multiplicity originate from that Brahman? It can only be an appearance; there is no real manifestation, no factual creation.

Verse 9

सच्चिदात्मन्यनुस्यूते नित्ये विष्णौ प्रकल्पिताः ।
व्यक्तयो विविधाः सर्वा हाटके कटकादिवत् ॥ ९ ॥

saccidātmanyanusyūte nitye viṣṇau prakalpitāḥ,
vyaktayo vividhāḥ sarvā hāṭake kaṭakādivat. (9)

सच्चिदात्मनि – in the Self whose nature is Existence-Consciousness; अनुस्यूते – in the all-pervading; नित्ये – in the eternal; विष्णौ – upon Viṣṇu; प्रकल्पिताः – projected by imagination; व्यक्तयः – manifested; विविधाः – manifold; सर्वाः – all; हाटके – out of gold; कटकादिवत् – just as bracelets and other ornaments

9. *The entire world of things and beings is only a mental projection upon the substratum which is the eternal all-pervading Viṣṇu, whose nature is Existence-Consciousness; just as, all the different ornaments are made out of the same gold.*

An ordinary gross mind can never lift itself to grasp easily the subtle truths of the highest Vedānta. Very frequently, innumerable examples are to be repeated to push the subtle philosophical ideas into the comprehension of an ordinary intellect. When they are quite apt, the students become pleasantly aghast at the revelations and the Truth becomes more and more clear to them.

In any creation there must be, as we have already noted, three fundamental and separate causes – (a) the material cause or the raw material, (b) the instrumental cause, the equipment with which the object is created and (c) the efficient cause, the intelligence that creates or works at the material with the instruments.

In all creations, the three causes exist separately and the material cause transforms itself into the created new thing; but in the case of the creation of the world, the objects created are not different from the Creator. The material cause, the one supreme Paramātman Himself manifests as different objects, for, in the infinitude of His existence, there cannot be a second infinite.

The waves in the ocean cannot claim a separate existence apart from the waters of the ocean. Likewise, this outer world and our own world of experiences in the physical, mental and intellectual spheres rise from, exist in, and merge back into that one supreme Awareness which glows in everybody, and like the bubbles that form and burst upon the surface of the water, different experiences in different hearts rise and fall before that one Consciousness.

Here 'Viṣṇu' is not to be understood as the four-armed divine deity of the Trinity, as the Purāṇas often describe. No doubt, when a gold ring goes out of shape or even when the ring is melted, nothing happens to gold. So too, even when the entire universe tumbles down, nothing happens to the eternal Reality since it is ever changeless and immutable.

Verse 10

यथाकाशो हृषीकेशो नानोपाधिगतो विभुः ।
तद्भेदाद्भिन्नवद्भाति तन्नाशे केवलो भवेत् ॥ १० ॥

yathākāśo hṛṣīkeśo nānopādhigato vibhuḥ,
tadbhedādbhinnavadbhāti tannāśe kevalo bhavet. (10)

यथा – just as; आकाशः – space; हृषीकेशः – the omnipresent Truth; नाना उपाधिगतः – associated with various conditionings; विभुः – the all-pervading; तत् भेदात् – on account of their manifold nature distinct from each other; भिन्नवत् भाति – appears to be diverse; तत् नाशे – on the destruction of these upādhis, केवलः – one; भवेत् – becomes

10. *The all-pervading space appears to be diverse on account of its association with various conditionings (upādhis) which are different from each other. However, upon the destruction of these limiting adjuncts the space becomes one. So also, the omnipresent Truth appears to be diverse on account of Its association with various upādhis and becomes one on the destruction of these upādhis.*

Behind all the apparent multiplicity of existence and the manifold nature of our experience, the one and the only changeless substratum persists in all its splendour. This alone is known as the Brahman, the Paramātman, the Sat-Cit-Ānanda and so on. This supreme Being alone is the dynamic Truth and no differentiation is possible in this state of absolute Reality. Then, how do we come to feel the plurality in the outer world of innumerable objects, which we experience now as so real? If the Spirit that pulsates through all the objects in and around us, is one without a second, why is this conflict being created by the perception of plurality in the outer world?

We discover the necessary courage to enquire in this fashion, because we are not prepared to accept all statements pertaining to Truth, merely because they had been declared by the ancient and the learned. Both our head and heart must assimilate any new idea before it can really become our own. Then alone can these philosophical ideas readily reach our heart to guide us in our day-to-day life and its transactions.

The word 'Hṛṣīkeśaḥ' can be interpreted both in its mythological tradition as well as in its ancient usage. Taking it as 'hṛṣ-keśa', it means one whose hair is made short. In the battlefield at Kurukṣetra we meet the Lord with all his curly hairs rolled up. In the ancient sense the term 'Hṛṣīkeśa' can be dissolved as 'hṛṣīka-īśa'. No doubt, 'hṛṣīka' is an old and obsolete word meaning sense organs and so the epithet means 'Lord of sense organs'. The sense organs can function, only so long as the life exists in us. As long as the Self, which is the Lord of the senses, reigns in this body, so long alone are we enabled to see, smell, touch, speak and so on. It is the one and only Spark of Life that pervades everything. Without this enlivening Spirit, nothing will operate in this body or exist in the world outside. That Principle of Life, that universal Spirit, that all-pervading Brahman is worthily known as 'Vibhuḥ', meaning, the all-pervading.

This all-pervading (Vibhuḥ) Truth, the Brahman, appears to be the pluralistic world, as stated before, because of the various conditionings through which It functions. For example, we construct different rooms in the vast open space (ākāśaḥ) and then we recognise distinct compartments in the one space as the drawing room, the bedroom, living room and so on, and then we ourselves come to treat the one (space) as a multiple factor. We consider the numerous small spaces created by such a division as so many different room spaces. But when the walls are pulled down, the room spaces having separate individual existence end, but thereby the space in none of them is destroyed. The room spaces become the one total space.

Similarly, when an individual ego associates with its various limiting factors (upādhis), this world of plurality comes to manifest. When these limiting factors are destroyed, the one dynamic Truth of life is rediscovered as that which functions through the entire existence. Without this Vibhu there is no existence and with It everything comes to exist.

The Ātman is one and the same before and after Realisation; but when It groans under certain imaginary limitations – all due to the wrong estimations of the distorting mind – we superimpose certain upādhis upon Ātman and when these false limitations are removed, It is realised and rediscovered as the one Self, ever dwelling everywhere.

Verse 11

नानोपाधिवशादेव जातिवर्णाश्रमादयः ।
आत्मन्यारोपितास्तोये रसवर्णादिभेदवत् ॥ ११ ॥

nānopādhivaśādeva jātivarṇāśramādayaḥ,
ātmanyāropitāstoye rasavarṇādibhedavat. (11)

नाना उपाधिवशात् – because of association with different conditionings (upādhis); एव – only; जातिवर्णाश्रमादयः – caste, colour, position and so on; आत्मनि – upon the Ātman; आरोपिताः – are superimposed; तोये – on water; रसवर्णादिभेदवत् – differences such as flavour, colour and so on

11. *Because of Its association with different conditionings (upādhis), the idea of caste, colour, position and so on, are superimposed upon the Ātman, just as flavour, colour and so on, are superimposed on water.*

Whether one is an advocate, a doctor or a porter, the inner personality factors are the same. The education gained, the apprenticeship undergone and the profession pursued are the only differences. They are all of one community – the community of man – but in their outer description and address, each differs from all others. Similarly, life is the same everywhere but the expression of life manifesting through each one of them differs from all others. Whatever be the physical shape and form, name or caste, emotional beauty or intellectual grasp exhibited, the Ātman is the same everywhere in all creatures. There is no difference such as a young Ātman, an old Ātman, a Christian Ātman, a Hindu Ātman, a poor Ātman, a rich Ātman and so on. The life-giving Truth in the varied existence of things is the one Reality, which equally thrills the entire panorama of things, persons and personalities. It remains unaffected by and unattached to all outward marks – always a dispassionate observer of the endless drama of life.

The same electric current causes the fan to revolve, the refrigerator to cool its contents, the light to burn differently in the green, blue or red bulbs. Because of the difference in the manifestations of the energy, as it passes through the different equipments, ignorant people call them by different names. Yet, the 'electricity wireman' understands them all as depending upon one energy.

Water itself is colourless although a given sample of it may be white, another yellow and yet another sample red, each depending upon the nature of the extraneous matter it contains. In the same way, according to the type of vāsanās in each individual, there seems to be difference between individuals. If we remove the contamination caused by the limitations (upādhis), understand and experience the one inner Spirit, which runs through all the individuals, we would realise that the difference we have been perceiving is merely a superimposition on that one glorious Reality, without whose illumination life would be dark and impossible, a non-existent nonentity.

Verse 12

पञ्चीकृतमहाभूतसम्भवं कर्मसञ्चितम् ।
शरीरं सुखदुःखानां भोगायतनमुच्यते ॥ १२ ॥

pañcīkṛtamahābhūtasambhavaṁ karmasañcitam,
śarīraṁ sukhaduḥkhānāṁ bhogāyatanamucyate. (12)

पञ्चीकृतमहाभूतसम्भवं – the five elements that have gone through the process of fivefold self division and mutual combination; कर्मसञ्चितम् – determined by one's own past actions; शरीरं – the gross body; सुखदुःखानां – for pleasure and pain; भोगायतनम् – medium of experiencing; उच्यते – is said

12. *Determined for each individual by his own past actions and made of the five elements – that have gone through the process of fivefold self division and mutual combination (pañcīkaraṇa) – is born the gross body, the medium through which pleasure and pain are experienced – the tenement of experiences.*

Now we come to analyse how the limiting factors or upādhis emerge – the biographical story of the growth and development of the 'bodies' or layers of matter beneath which the Ātman revels as luminous Consciousness. The three bodies are known as the gross, the subtle and the causal body.

The gross body is composed of the five elements – space, air, fire, water and earth. Observe the history of the body during its disintegration after death – soon after life has departed from it – the heat contents pass out and the body becomes icy cold (fire), it also bloats up and emits gas (air), and soon it decays in its own juicy contents (water) and finally, the bare physical structure decays to dust (earth). The space occupied by the body is yielded back (space).

Every creation is a manifestation of the gross from the prior subtle state and we all know that the cause precedes the effect. In the theory of pañcīkaraṇa it is very elaborately pointed out how these five elements are evolved, how they intermingle and how from the subtle tanmātrās, the gross elements are formed.

The five great elements are space, air, fire, water and earth. Before grossification, they exist in their pure form – each by themselves – and hence they are known as tanmātrā (literally 'that alone'). Their grossification takes place in five definite scientific stages –

Stage 1: They remain in their own individual pure state.

Stage 2: Each tanmātrā of all the five elements shows a tendency to split into two equal halves.

Stage 3: They split into two halves.

Stage 4: At this stage half tanmātrā of each element remains intact and the other half divides itself into four equal bits, each bit being one-eighth of the whole tanmātrā. Thus, at this stage each tanmātrā (of stage 1) has split into five segments, one-half bit and four one-eighth bits.

Stage 5: In this last stage, each half remains the same and it combines with the four one-eighth bits borrowed from all other remaining four elements, thus becoming gross.

PAÑCĪKARAṆA

The Process of fivefold self-division and mutual combination

Stage	Space 1	Air 2	Fire 3	Water 4	Earth 5	Description
(i)						Tanmātrās; each in itself.
(ii)						Tendency to divide into two equal parts.
(iii)						The split complete.
(iv)	0000	0000	0000	0000	0000	One half remaining intact the other half splits into 4 equal parts.
(v)	2 3 4 5	1 3 4 5	1 2 4 5	1 2 3 5	1 2 3 4	Each half combines with 4-bits borrowed from all others.

Space	= ½ S	+ 1/8 A	+ 1/8 F	+ 1/8 W	+ 1/8 E
Air	= ½ A	+ 1/8 S	+ 1/8 F	+ 1/8 W	+ 1/8 E
Fire	= ½ F	+ 1/8 S	+ 1/8 A	+ 1/8 W	+ 1/8 E
Water	= ½ W	+ 1/8 S	+ 1/8 A	+ 1/8 F	+ 1/8 E
Earth	= ½ E	+ 1/8 S	+ 1/8 A	+ 1/8 F	+ 1/8 W

The human body as already stated is the equipment with which we perceive things and it is with the sense organs available in the body that we derive our quota of pleasure and pain, which in their turn give us a measure of success and failure in our individual lives.

The enjoyment of pleasure and pain (bhoga) in this physical body – the hut of pleasure, the hall of experience – is determined by our past karmas. Thought by thought, action by action, we have demanded the present body and mental equipment. In fact, even while we are alive and acting here at present, we order the shape of the future life to be. Unless we conquer the bad vāsanās by right conduct and practise systematically the righteous values of life, we do not come to live in an atmosphere in which our thoughts and actions are sufficiently divine to be directly helpful for our own progressive evolution. It, therefore, now rests with us to make or mar our progress – to get a better life with plenty of opportunities in which we can slowly and steadily go forward and ultimately come to realise the supreme Truth or to get a wicked life in which we can dive ourselves into a greater gloom. With our own actions we give a blueprint to God ordering the exact shape of our destiny and according to the specifications given, the body, the tenement of experiences, is built and handed over to each one of us by the all-merciful, omnipotent, divine Creator.

Verse 13

पञ्चप्राणमनोबुद्धिदशेन्द्रियसमन्वितम् ।
अपञ्चीकृतभूतोत्थं सूक्ष्माङ्गं भोगसाधनम् ॥ १३ ॥

pañcaprāṇamanobuddhidaśendriyasamanvitam,
apañcīkṛtabhūtottham sūkṣmāṅgam bhogasādhanam. (13)

पञ्चप्राणमनोबुद्धिदशेन्द्रियसमन्वितम् – the five prāṇas, mind, intellect and the ten organs combined; अपञ्चीकृतभूतोत्थं – formed from the rudimentary elements; सूक्ष्माङ्गं – the subtle body; भोगसाधनम् – instrument of experience

13. *The subtle body, which is the instrument of experience is constituted of five prāṇas, the ten organs, the mind and intellect, formed from the rudimentary elements (tanmātrās) as they exist before their fivefold division and mutual combination with one another (pañcīkaraṇa).*

In the lower wombs such as the plants and the animals and the higher ones like the humans and the celestials, there are vast differences. But behind all these wonderful differences, to any discriminative intellect capable of seeing things in their correct and true perspective, there is one pulsating force that plays the song of life through all these various equipments. If there be such a oneness of existence everywhere, why is there a series of different experiences within myself and why then, again the various grades of life outside? Vedānta has not only theoretically dealt with this question but a practical approach has been made to this problem. A very convincing answer indeed is given to this deep doubt.

In this verse the term 'prāṇa' is to be correctly understood. It is not mechanical breathing in and out. It is the manifestation of life in our body and the five prāṇas are the five departments of life's activities or categories of prāṇa functioning departmentally in five ways.

They are – (1) Prāṇa is that Life Force which controls and regulates the various activities of our sense organs. It is because of this dynamic energy that life is evident in sense perceptions; (2) apāna is the excretory system in a healthy body – the capacity to reject the unnecessary and unwanted poisonous things from the body; (3) samāna expresses life's functions in the digestive system, which makes the food ready for absorption by the body; (4) vyāna distributes the digested food with equity and justice, as the very word indicated, according to the need of the moment to each part. More food goes to our hands if we are cutting wood or breaking stones and more for the legs if we are running or walking; (5) udāna is the capacity to rise up and peep into fresh fields of knowledge by which the existing wrong notions are removed by the newly acquired convictions and experiences; it is the capacity in us to evolve or devolve in our thoughts.

As the one Central Government holds its sway over the whole country from its seat in New Delhi, so too the one Self, the Life Principle seated in the heart cave has its sway over the whole body while it functions from the heart cave. The governance of the body is conducted through the different prāṇas that are referred to above; just as any government would have its various ministers. One Life Principle alone expresses itself in its five different moods and each performs a different function in the physical body as each minister is in charge of a given department and all of them are expressions of the one government in power.

Prāṇa controls the perceptions of the different sense organs. The spots on the physical body at which sense perceptions seem to function are not in themselves the sense organs. For instance, the two eyes are only instruments (golakas) through which the power of vision beams forth and the exact power of vision is in essence located in the mind-intellect equipment. If the mind does not come in contact with the sense organs, perception is not possible. A man in deep thoughts or sleep does not see and recognise the person standing by his side, because his mind has not gone out through the eyes to see the object before him[1].

This subtle body constituted of the five prāṇas, the ten organs, the mind and the intellect – the instruments with which we experience pain and pleasure, is made out of the five great elements, called the rudimentary elements (tanmātrās), before they have gone through the process of their fivefold subdivision and mutual combination (pañcīkaraṇa). The physical body explained in the previous verse is an establishment serving as the hall of experience, the subtle body formed out of the rudimentary elements (tanmātrās) is that by which or through which the enjoyment of the objects in the outer world is rendered possible. The subtle body is constituted of the instruments of experience.

[1] In Vedānta the theory of perception is that the Consciousness riding over the mind flows through the sense organs and reaches the object (ghata-deśa) and takes the shape of the object. Then we gain the knowledge (vṛtti-jñānam) that this is the object (ayam ghaṭaḥ).

Verse 14

अनाद्यविद्यानिर्वाच्या कारणोपाधिरुच्यते ।
उपाधित्रितयादन्यमात्मानमवधारयेत् ॥ १४ ॥

anādyavidyānirvācyā kāraṇopādhirucyate,
upādhitritayādanyamātmānamavadhārayet. (14)

अनाद्यविद्या – beginningless ignorance; अनिर्वाच्या – indescribable; कारणोपाधिः – causal body; उच्यते – is said; उपाधित्रितयात् अन्यम् – other than the three conditioning bodies; आत्मानम् – the Ātman; अवधारयेत् – should understand

14. *Avidyā which is indescribable and beginningless is the causal body. Know for certain that the Ātman is other than these three conditioning bodies (upādhis).*

In all cases of delusory superimpositions such as a ghost-vision in a post, the cause for the illusion is in the accidental non-apprehension of the reality. When Truth is not known (avidyā), when the reality of a thing is veiled (āvaraṇa) from us, we cannot but misinterpret the reality through our own misdirected imaginations (vikṣepa), which form the delusory projections (adhyāsa). When the intellect is clouded with ignorance, the mind dances in agitation, painting for itself an exhaustive picture of dark despair.

When the Spirit is not known due to the veiling layers of ignorance (avidyā), the misapprehensions of the Spirit as the various matter envelopments start. Identifying with these layers, the delusory sense of individuality arises and this ego suffers the pains and agonies of existence (saṁsāra). The mere non-apprehension, in case it is not creating any misapprehensions is a condition of relative joy.[1]

This avidyā is the causal body, inasmuch as it is this ignorance of an eternal spiritual perfection that has given us our gurgling desires in the intellect, thoughts in the mind and actions through the body. The subtle body and gross body are the products of avidyā and, therefore, avidyā is known as the causal body.

Beginningless (anādi) – This is a description of this mysterious avidyā, which the students of Vedānta, in their early days of study find very difficult to accept and assimilate. Clear light is thrown into this concept by the modern revelations in science.

Time, according to modern scientists, is the interval between events. In textbooks of philosophical thoughts, a more vivid definition is given which perhaps has a closer personal appeal – time is the interval between experiences. To have an experience three factors are necessary – the experiencer (subject), the experienced (object) and the right relationship established and maintained between the subject and the object, known as the experiencing. Thus, the mind-intellect instrument, the experiencer, must have a world of objects, the experienced, to establish the condition of experiencing to have the first experience.

[1] In the 'joyless joy-state' of deep sleep we are in pure avidyā, in sheer non-apprehension of both, Self and the not-Self.

At a single point A, there is no distance to measure; but from point A to any point B, there is a distance. When the first experience ends, which is at the rise of a different experience, then alone can the concept of first unit of time appear in our comprehension.

Even for the very first experience, where time is impossible, we need the equipments of the mind and intellect as well as the world of objects to perceive, feel and think. Thus, even before time was perceived, the created world must have come out and to perceive it the equipments of knowledge also must have been created. Avidyā is the causal body for the subtle and gross envelopments and, therefore, it cannot be qualified or measured by 'time' which is its own by-product. So often the grandson complains, 'Grandpa, why did you not take me to the marriage of my granny?' Avidyā is before time – anādi, that is timeless.

This avidyā is again qualified here by Śaṅkara as indescribable. A thing that exists and which can be an object of our perception, feeling or thought; that alone can be framed in expressions and explained or described. But avidyā which is the cause for the instruments of perception, feeling and thought, cannot be brought fully within our experience and hence the difficulty to explain it. Again, if a thing exists it can be explained, a non-existent thing also can be explained; avidyā can neither be said to be existent nor non-existent (or both), and therefore, it is inexplicable.

Lastly, in Vedānta the theme of discussion is vidyā and not avidyā. The seeker has come to the Teacher seeking Knowledge, not ignorance. Therefore, the śāstra says that the seekers need not try to understand and experience ignorance, it is impossible to do so; with a torch, however fast we may run we will never be able to see darkness. Night flies before the vivid rays of the morning. Keeping a burning gaslight on his head, one fool once walked the whole night through, trying to place that light at some place where there is darkness! He failed. The more we try to understand or know ignorance, the more it moves off until we reach true knowledge.

Verse 15

पञ्चकोशादियोगेन तत्तन्मय इव स्थितः ।
शुद्धात्मा नीलवस्त्रादियोगेन स्फटिको यथा ॥ १५ ॥

pañcakośādiyogena tattanmaya iva sthitaḥ,
śuddhātmā nīlavastrādiyogena sphaṭiko yathā. (15)

पञ्चकोशादियोगेन – by identification with the five sheaths and so on; तत् – that; तन्मय – identical with that; इव – like; स्थितः – appears; शुद्धात्मा – the pure Self; नीलवस्त्रादियोगेन – association with blue garment and so on; स्फटिकः – crystal; यथा – just as

15. *In Its identifications with the five sheaths, the immaculate Ātman appears to have borrowed their qualities upon Itself, as in the case of a crystal which appears blue or yellow depending upon the colour of the cloth in its vicinity.*

Here, we are given an answer as to how the perfect, the immaculate Self happens to be contaminated by the impure and the imperfect. The Self is ever pure and the same everywhere and It is never contaminated by the finite objects of creation or by the different layers of matter, which are the products of the non-apprehension of the Truth. However, when life is expressed through the mind and the sense organs, we seem to wrongly imagine that this unchanging Supreme, because of Its association with the imperfect objects and due to the conditionings (upādhis) gathers to Itself the stink of the five sheaths[1]. The venom of the superimposed serpent cannot poison the rope, its substratum; the blood on the lips of the ghost can never leave any stain upon the innocent post.

A clear glass tumbler seems to take up the colour of the table cloth on which it happens to stand. Similarly, because of the seeming identification and association of the pure Self with the five sheaths, expressing Itself in and through them, we mistakenly identify the five sheaths as our true nature.

The five sheaths are – (a) the gross physical structure, the anatomical (annamaya), (b) the vital air sheath, the physiological (prāṇamaya), (c) the mental sheath, the psychological (manomaya), (d) the intellectual sheath (vijñānamaya) and (e) the bliss sheath (ānandamaya).

[1] The personality of an individual is analysed into five layers on the basis of their distinct functions and these are known as the pañca-kośas, the five sheaths. They are: annamaya kośa (food sheath); prāṇamaya kośa (vital air sheath); manomaya kośa (mental sheath); vijñānamaya kośa (intellectual sheath) and ānandamaya kośa (bliss sheath).

Verse 16

वपुस्तुषादिभिः कोशैर्युक्तं युक्त्यावघाततः ।
आत्मानमन्तरं शुद्धं विविच्यात्तण्डुलं यथा ॥ १६ ॥

vapustuṣādibhiḥ kośairyuktaṁ yuktyāvaghātataḥ,
ātmānamantaraṁ śuddhaṁ vivicyāttaṇḍulaṁ yathā. (16)

वपुस्तुषादिभिः – the form with husk and so on; कोशैः – with sheaths; युक्तं – covered; युक्त्या – by logical thinking; अवघाततः – by thrashing rice in a mortar; आत्मानम् – the Self; अन्तरं – within; शुद्धम् – pure; विविच्यात् – should separate; तण्डुलं – rice; यथा – just as

16. *Through discriminative self-analysis and logical thinking one should separate the pure Self within, from the sheaths, as one separates the rice from the husk, bran and so on, that are covering it.*

Then, how are we to visualise the glory and greatness of this all-pervading, supreme Truth which is the Self in us? How do we separate Spirit from matter and realise the pure Spirit?

Rice is obtained by removing the husk, bran and so on, from the paddy. In the same way, using 'viveka', the faculty of discriminating the Real from the unreal, one has to differentiate the Self from the layers of the not-Self – that cover and dim the light of the real Self – and then come to realise the Self in its pure and uncontaminated state.

Thus, by the art of negation of the physical and mental equipments in us and also by the removal of the dirt that has been let in to rest on that Immortal, the glory of the total existence in the manifold creation, the Ātman, is to be realised as the pure Consciousness. When an earnest seeker subjectively experiences this Truth, he becomes detached from the various sheaths, which are his personality layers. He realises that the soul is different from those layers and in the constant process of detachment from them, he attains the infinite Knowledge and the absolute bliss, he rediscovers his spiritual status as the eternal Self.

Verse 17

सदा सर्वगतोऽप्यात्मा न सर्वत्रावभासते ।
बुद्धावेवावभासेत स्वच्छेषु प्रतिबिम्बवत् ॥ १७ ॥

sadā sarvagato'pyātmā na sarvatrāvabhāsate,
buddhāvevāvabhāseta svaccheṣu pratibimbavat. (17)

सदा – always; सर्वगतः – all-pervading; अपि – although; आत्मा – the Self; न – not; सर्वत्र – everywhere; अवभासते – shines; बुद्धौ – in the intellect; एव – only; अवभासेत – manifests; स्वच्छेषु – in the transparent surface; प्रतिबिम्बवत् – just as the reflection

17. *The Ātman does not shine in everything although it is all-pervading. It manifests only in the inner equipment, the intellect (buddhi), just as the reflection in a clean mirror.*

The Ātman, being infinite, is by Its very nature all-pervading. Although it is available in the cognition of all objects, in the pure intellect (buddhi) alone can we come to realise the Self (Ātmā) in all its essential splendour; just as, in a clear polished mirror alone are we able to see our reflections distinctly, although according to the principles of reflection[1] our faces are reflected everywhere on all objects.

[1] According to physics, light falling on the object gets reflected and these reflected light rays again get reflected at the reflecting surface; and when they fall on our retina we see the reflection. This process goes on even on a granite rough wall surface but we don't see our reflection there.

Let us again take the example of our own government. It functions from New Delhi but it sounds odd if we really mean that the government is in New Delhi alone and not in the other parts of India. The government may have its headquarters up in the north but even in a little home far away in the south, the overall hold and grace of the government falls equally. On every inch of the country it has its sway. Its laws are applicable throughout the length and breadth of the land. Yet, to meet the government one must go to New Delhi. So too, although the Lord, the supreme Brahman, who is the substratum of all the plurality within and without, it is only in the subtle intellect (buddhi), purified and steadied, that It is fully reflected and seen clearly.

The body is gross, the mind is agitated over one thing or another and hence it is through the subtle intellect alone that one can learn to be calm and steady, albeit by practice. In that serene quietude of a settled and pure mind, the effulgent Self is recognised, just as we can see quite easily and clearly, our own image only in a clean mirror held steady.

Verse 18

देहेन्द्रियमनोबुद्धिप्रकृतिभ्यो विलक्षणम्।
तद्वृत्तिसाक्षिणं विद्यादात्मानं राजवत्सदा ॥ १८ ॥

dehendriyamanobuddhiprakṛtibhyo vilakṣaṇam,
tadvṛttisākṣiṇaṁ vidyādātmānaṁ rājavatsadā. (18)

देहेन्द्रियमनोबुद्धिप्रकृतिभ्यः – from the body, senses, mind and intellect constituting the matter (prakṛti); विलक्षणम् – distinct; तद्वृत्तिसाक्षिणं – witness of their functions; विद्यात् – know; आत्मानं – the Self; राजवत् – like a king; सदा – always

18. *One should understand that the Ātman is always like the king, distinct from the body, senses, mind and intellect, which constitute the matter (prakṛti) and It is the witness of their functions.*

The pure Intelligence, the all-pervading Brahman is to be understood as distinct from and beyond the physical equipments constituted of the body, mind and intellect; for it is the supreme Illuminator which illumines the subtle workings of the intellect, the gross thoughts of the mind and the even grosser physical movements. In spite of all this seemingly interesting association and illumination It is ever a mere witness and never a participant. An illuminator is always separate from the objects illumined; the subject of experience cannot be the same as the objects of the same experience.

A king is not a participant in the drama and dance in his royal court. He is only a witness, and like him the Ātman is a witness of the drama of life going on in this body and in the world outside – the microcosmic and the macrocosmic existence.

Subjectively analysed, the Self is a witness of the play of matter, the good and bad ideas, the knowledge of right and wrong, the feeling of sorrow and joy, the appreciation of beauty and ugliness, our sense of duty and neglect and so on, and the actions of the physical body are all aspects of our inner and outer subjective life. These experiences, constituted of the knowledge of what we know and also of those that we do not know, for example, the positive experience of a thing and the nothingness of what we do not know – the bhāva and the abhāva – are all illumined by that one Awareness, the pure Consciousness. It stands aloof and does not identify with what is happening in the entire cosmic order, nor does It identify with what is happening within ourselves in the different layers of matter. It is not the sharer of the experience; It is only an observer like the king in his royal court, a non-partisan in all affairs, disinterested in all happenings and yet all-powerful (rājavat).

Verse 19

व्यापृतेष्विन्द्रियेष्वात्मा व्यापारीवाविवेकिनाम् ।
दृश्यतेऽभ्रेषु धावत्सु धावन्निव यथा शशी ॥ १९ ॥

vyāpṛteṣvindriyeṣvātmā vyāpārīvāvivekinām,
dṛśyate'bhreṣu dhāvatsu dhāvanniva yathā śaśī. (19)

व्यापृतेषु – while functioning; इन्द्रियेषु – the sense organs; आत्मा – the Self; व्यापारी – active; इव – like; अविवेकिनाम् – for non-discriminating person; दृश्यते – appears; अभ्रेषु – the clouds; धावत्सु – that are moving; धावन् इव – as though running; यथा – just as; शशी – the moon

19. *The moon appears to be running when the clouds move in the sky. Likewise, to the non-discriminating person, the Ātman appears to be active when it is observed through the functions of the sense organs.*

When the imperishable Self sheds Its illumination and expresses Itself in the life of the perishable individual, it looks as though the Self Itself is acting. The actions and movements are of the sense organs (indriyas) – not of the Self, the Life Spark in us, which is the sole nourisher of all life. It gives the organs their capacities for such manifestations.

The steam in the engine supplies the power for the locomotive to pull the train of carriages. It has neither a favour for, nor any prejudice against, anybody travelling in the attached compartments. The steam has no particular destination to reach. Similarly, when the supreme Ātman expresses Itself through the body, mind and intellect, the Self seems to act, but actually the Self participates in none of the activities of the sheaths; It has nothing to gain through any such activities.

So, whatever thoughts and actions spark up within and fly past a given individual, the Self alone is the substratum for all of them and it is in the light of the Self that they are recognised and experienced. There would be absolutely no manifestation or existence of life, either in the individual or in the cosmic order, without the omnipotence of this supreme Self, available ever so readily to sustain them.

A person who lacks in his powers of discrimination (avivekī) does not perceive the Truth playing so evidently beneath the play of manifested life but mistakes the activity of the not-Self as that of the Self, even though the Self perceptibly remains only as an unbiased witness and a detached observer.

In almost each one of the verses, we are given a comparison without which the mighty and glorious existence of the real Self cannot be indicated as the immaculate, ever uncontaminated by the frolics of the unreal. Here, the illustration is that of the moon, which seems to the childish folk as moving because of the clouds that pass in front of it. In a train journey it looks as though the trees and hillocks of the country side are moving fast, while actually, it is indeed the train that is moving. Through a moving medium, even a motionless steady object looks as though moving. The objects observed gather to themselves the properties of the medium through which we observe.

The illustration employed here has a very deep significance to those who can clearly meditate upon it. The entire import of the illustration can strike us down with a joyful amazement when we visualise the picture clearly. Imagine an observer from the surface of the vast earth, who is six feet tall, looking up at the moon that glows thousands of miles away, through clouds that are a few miles away from him. And yet, the observer cries, 'The cloud has covered the moon' or 'The moon is running'. Similarly, the infinite Self, when viewed through the restlessness of the body, mind and intellect, looks as though agitated and active.

If there be the sufficient mental poise and the required scientific observation of the phenomena of life, the intelligent student can easily recognise that all agitations belong, in fact, to the matter layers in us and the Self is never involved in them. The moon seems to be moving, because we look at it through a moving medium.

We recognise life as dynamic, because we observe it only through the vehicles of its expressions. Looking at a living creature, through its physical, mental and intellectual activities, we say life is dynamic, active, ever pulsating. In fact, life as such is not active, the vehicles thrilled by life act and these actions are superimposed upon the Self and in this confused observation it seems as though the Self is active.

When the mind is agitated, the Self seems to be agitated. We do not realise that the Self has no such agitations, that It is silent and steady, firm and dispassionate and that these eruptions are only on the surface of the mind. Thus, upon the glorious Self are wrongly superimposed the functions of the different layers of matter. To experience the Self, without the intervention of the matter sheaths, is to realise Its infinite divinity.

Verse 20

आत्मचैतन्यमाश्रित्य देहेन्द्रियमनोधियः ।
स्वक्रियार्थेषु वर्तन्ते सूर्यालोकं यथा जनाः ॥ २० ॥

ātmacaitanyamāśritya dehendriyamanodhiyaḥ,
svakriyārtheṣu vartante sūryālokaṁ yathā janāḥ. (20)

आत्मचैतन्यम् – Self which is of the nature of Consciousness; आश्रित्य – depending upon; देहेन्द्रियमनोधियः – body, senses, mind and intellect; स्वक्रियार्थेषु – in their respective activities; वर्तन्ते – engage; सूर्यालोकं – light of the sun; यथा – just as; जनाः – people

20. *Depending upon the Ātman which is of the nature of Consciousness, the body, senses, mind and intellect engage themselves in their respective activities, just as men work depending upon the light of the sun.*

All the equipments – body, mind and intellect – function in their own definite sphere and each one of them depends entirely upon that power (Ātma-caitanya), which by Its mere presence kindles life in matter and makes it look as though sentient.

The power of electricity is one but its fields of operation are different. Without electricity, even if we have all the bulbs and switches in their proper places, we do not get any manifestations. Likewise, without the enlivening Ātman, no activity is possible in this world. Without its grace, the entire created world of objects would be dead inert matter devoid of life. It is the Ātman, the Self which makes up the life in all, at once dynamic, gay, energetic and beaming with attraction, although in Itself, the Self is not affected by the things and happenings of life, which It illumines in Its shining, divine presence.

The illustration here is that of the various activities that start with the rising of the sun in the east. Whatever be the thoughts and actions of an individual who faces the day, the sun which illumines the earth, is not affected by the happiness or sorrow of those who are here in this world. It simply illumines whatever part of the globe that comes before its power of illumination. So too, at the touch of the illumining glory of the Self (Ātma-caitanya), the outer world of activities is vitalised. The Self never gets mixed up with anything which It vitalises. Whatever be the situation which the sun is illumining – some bleeding war or some boiling tar – the sun neither gets red nor black – the sunlight need never get boiled up with the prevailing sense of hate or heat.

Verse 21

देहेन्द्रियगुणान्कर्माण्यमले सच्चिदात्मनि ।
अध्यस्यन्त्यविवेकेन गगने नीलतादिवत् ॥ २१ ॥

dehendriyaguṇānkarmāṇyamale saccidātmani,
adhyasyantyavivekena gagane nīlatādivat. (21)

देहेन्द्रियगुणान्कर्माणि – qualities and functions of the body and senses; अमले – pure; सत् चित् आत्मनि – on the Self of the nature of Existence-Knowledge; अध्यस्यन्ति – superimpose; अविवेकेन – by lack of discrimination; गगने – in the sky; नीलतादिवत् – blue colour and the like

21. *Fools, because they lack in their powers of discrimination, superimpose on the Self of the nature of absolute Existence-Knowledge (Sat-Cit), all the varied functions of the body and the senses, just as they attribute blue colour and the like to the sky.*

Since they lack in their powers of right discrimination, the ignorant superimpose the qualities of the body, mind, intellect and the limitations of the physical and subtle body upon the pure Self. Thereafter, the deluded mistake the real Self to be one possessing all the imperfections of the superimposed equipments. This non-discrimination (aviveka) is like the misconception which makes children believe that sky is blue, although it has no colour.

Not only the blueness, but also its concavity, murkiness, misty looks and dusty conditions are all often considered as conditions of the sky. In fact, sky appears to be having these qualities but the sky as such has none of them.

An object is not affected by the traits superimposed upon it and here, when we superimpose certain characteristics of the body and mind on the self-effulgent Being, the Truth itself is not affected by such misconceived notions and attributes. The blueness perceived is the experience of our limited vision when it looks at the endless summer sky.

Verse 22

अज्ञानान्मानसोपाधेः कर्तृत्वादीनि चात्मनि ।
कल्प्यन्तेऽम्बुगते चन्द्रे चलनादि यथाम्भसः ॥ २२ ॥

ajñānānmānasopādheḥ kartṛtvādīni cātmani,
kalpyante'mbugate candre calanādi yathāmbhasaḥ. (22)

अज्ञानात् – due to ignorance; मानसोपाधेः – of the mind which is a upādhi; कर्तृत्वादीनि – agency of actions and so on; च – and; आत्मनि – on the Self; कल्प्यन्ते – attributed; अम्बुगते – which is reflected in the water; चन्द्रे – in the moon; चलनादि – tremblings and so on; यथा – just as; अम्भसः – of the water

22. *Due to ignorance, the tremblings that belong to the water are attributed to the reflected moon dancing on it, likewise the agency of actions and so on, are delusively understood as the nature of the Self (Ātman).*

The ideas such as 'I am the enjoyer', 'I am the doer' are of the intellect. These different ideas, such as 'I am this', 'I am that' and so on, rise in the mind-intellect only when we are in the midst of the activities of waking and dreamworld; for, when we are in deep sleep we do not have any such ideas. It is only when the mind is available for perception and cognition that we come to know of the things cognised. As long as we identify ourselves with the mind, so long alone can we claim to have the dual experiences in these planes of existence. Once we have withdrawn ourselves from the mental plane and are in a state of pure Consciousness (samādhi), we realise that all the thoughts, emotions and activities of the intellect, mind and body are not in the Self, nor are they of the Self. The delusory reflection of the Consciousness in the mental pool which agitates, with the panting egoistic ideas of 'I am the doer', 'I am the enjoyer' and so on, cease when there are no more thought eruptions therein.

The example in this verse is of an image of the moon reflected in a bucket of water which seems to shiver when the water surface is disturbed. When the water calms down and becomes steady, we do not see the shattered moon but reassembling to form one whole. Similarly, when one has purified one's mind, consolidated its strength, and reconstructed it to be firm and steady by narrowing down its various unholy, unhelpful and selfish thoughts, the glory of the Self gets automatically reflected in all its beauty within oneself, unshaken by the dualities around and the consequent agitations.

Verse 23

**रागेच्छासुखदुःखादि बुद्धौ सत्यां प्रवर्तते ।
सुषुप्तौ नास्ति तन्नाशे तस्माद्बुद्धेस्तु नात्मनः ॥ २३ ॥**

rāgecchāsukhaduḥkhādi buddhau satyāṁ pravartate,
suṣuptau nāsti tannāśe tasmādbuddhestu nātmanaḥ. (23)

रागेच्छासुखदुःखादि – attachment, desire, pleasure, pain and so on; बुद्धौ सत्यां – when mind or intellect functions; प्रवर्तते – are perceived; सुषुप्तौ – in deep sleep; न – not; अस्ति – is; तत् नाशे – upon its destruction; तस्मात् – therefore; बुद्धेः – of the mind; तु – only; न – not; आत्मनः – of the Ātman

23. *Attachment, desire, pleasure, pain and so on, are perceived to exist only as long as the mind or intellect functions. They are not perceived in deep sleep when the mind ceases to exist. Therefore, they belong to the mind alone and not the Ātman.*

There is no place for ignorance in the blissful existence of the Self which is omniscient and omnipresent. How can there be darkness before light, and how can the passions that arise in the mind come to stay with the Ātman? It is the avidyā of the individual – his desires for pleasure and attachment to the fruits of his actions – that deludes him to the bondage of saṁsāra.

A pure mind leads one to greater glory and happiness and ultimately to Liberation through the final experience of the true knowledge, whilst the same mind drags the individual down to lower births, when it groans in ajñāna. Therefore, if we deal suitably with the turbulent mind and quieten its riotous activities, the Self is revealed in Its infinite glory with no blemish of the jīvātmā in Him – because attachment, desire and so on, are of the mind and not of the Ātman.

So long as we are functioning through our mind, we are under the tyranny of attachment, desire, pleasure, pain and so on, but in deep sleep when our minds are temporarily ineffective, all these tyrannies are not experienced. When I look through a pair of green goggles everything looks green. When I look at things with my naked eye, there is no green colour. Therefore, the greenness is due to the glasses.

Verse 24

प्रकाशोऽर्कस्य तोयस्य शैत्यमग्नेर्यथोष्णता ।
स्वभावः सच्चिदानन्दनित्यनिर्मलतात्मनः ॥ २४ ॥

prakāśo'rkasya toyasya śaityamagneryathoṣṇatā,
svabhāvaḥ saccidānandanityanirmalatātmanaḥ. (24)

प्रकाशः – luminosity; अर्कस्य – of the sun; तोयस्य – for water; शैत्यम् – coolness; अग्नेः – for fire; यथा – just as; उष्णता – heat; स्वभावः – nature; सच्चिदानन्दनित्यनिर्मलतात्मनः – Existence-Consciousness-Bliss, Eternity, Purity of the Ātman

24. *Just as luminosity is the nature of the sun, coolness is that of water and heat is that of fire, so too, the nature of the Ātman is Eternity, Purity, Existence, Consciousness and Bliss.*

Whether it is the human personality or the plant specimen or animal entity, no one wants to die or suffer any agony and pain. Instead, there is a positive effort at all times for the acquisition of knowledge and the enjoyment of pleasure and for the self-preservation of the individuality.

Nothing can remain away from its dharma (essential nature) – there cannot be cool fire or a dark sun. Every object must express its own essential nature.

The sun is luminosity itself and this is amply evident from its effulgence. The heat of the fire is well-known and no one has come across a cold ball of fire. Similarly, if at all Ātman is to be defined in terms of its nature we can only say that it is that which is eternal (nitya), ever pure (nirmala) and Existence-Consciousness-Bliss (Sat-Cit-Ānanda).

Verse 25

आत्मनः सच्चिदंशश्च बुद्धेर्वृत्तिरिति द्वयम् ।
संयोज्य चाविवेकेन जानामीति प्रवर्तते ॥ २५ ॥

ātmanaḥ saccidaṁśaśca buddhervṛttiriti dvayam,
saṁyojya cāvivekena jānāmīti pravartate. (25)

आत्मनः – of the Self; सच्चिदंशः – the Existence-Consciousness aspect; च – and; बुद्धेः – of the intellect; वृत्तिः – the thought wave; इति – thus; द्वयम् – the two; संयोज्य – blending; च – and; अविवेकेन – through indiscrimination; जानामि – I know; इति – thus; प्रवर्तते – functions

25. *By the indiscriminate blending of the two, the Existence-Consciousness aspects of the Self and the thought wave of the intellect, there arises the notion of 'I know'.*

The Ātman is self effulgent, whereas the mind is inert matter. Without the power of illumination in Consciousness, the mind would be inert and powerless to feel, for without this Awareness within we will not be conscious of our own thoughts. At the same time a marriage between these two contradictory things is impossible, and therefore, any alliance between the two is at best only a delusory superimposition.

The experience 'I know' is thus produced only when a feeling or thought stands bathed in the light of Consciousness. Each thought is considered as a wave like disturbance in the mental pool. When these waves of thoughts arise in us, they are illumined by our awareness; then we cry 'I know', 'I understand', 'I feel' and so on.

The sun rises, and then the waves of the sea are seen and experienced. The sunlight falls on all surfaces equally. Like a silken veil it lies on every surface and when the waves rise the light veil yields, embracing the waves on all sides and illumining them. So too in our inner heart, the light of Consciousness illumines the height, breadth and depth of each thought.

The mind-intellect equipment stands ever exposed to the eternal Self and its light of Awareness. Through the sense organs, when the stimuli from external world reach the heart, the mind with the help of the knowledge acquired by it in the past, produces its responses, which in their turn are expressed in the actions. Life is an unbroken series of experiences, and therefore, the individual is called upon to respond to it constantly. To know the happenings and to know how to meet them is the very purpose of man's intellectual life.

Self is Knowledge Absolute, It is Knowledge itself. In it there is nothing else that is to be known. It is the only one subject without any object to be known. As such, in Itself, the Self has nothing to know. Yet, we are experiencing the intellectual life of constantly knowing. How? This is the subject explained in this verse.

It is the theory in Vedānta that the knowledge of things is gained not in the direct light of Consciousness, but it is in the beam of Consciousness reflected in the mind. I will explain it with the help of an illustration. Suppose there is a storeroom in your house which is ever in darkness. One day you realised that the room was extremely well illumined. Why? There was a bucket of water on the verandah where the sunlight got reflected and threw a pool of light on the dark wall of the room. If your little son were to come at that time to play with the bucket of water, the illumination in the dark room will disappear; for, when the reflecting medium is disturbed and the reflected light is splashed about, the room is again in the dark until the reflection rehabilitates itself on the wall.

So too, the Self never illumines the objects directly but the light of Consciousness reflected on the intellect throws out a beam of reflected Consciousness which illumines the objects and gives us the experience 'I know'. That is why even a man of intelligence, when vexed with some worries, cannot think properly or understand easily. His power of understanding or thinking is clouded when the mind is disturbed.

Thus, when the mental pool rises in thought waves, the light of the Self illumines them. Thought dressed in Consciousness is the clear experience 'I know'. Feelings and ideas in our bosom glittering in Consciousness are our knowledge of things.

Anger, knowledge and so on, are all characteristics of the mind and they are attributed to the Ātman due to lack of discrimination. The nature of the Ātman, in reality, is Sat-Cit-Ānanda and this eternal Self does not undergo any change even when the individual experiences anger, pain, pleasure and so on, in his mind.

Verse 26

आत्मनो विक्रिया नास्ति बुद्धेर्बोधो न जात्विति ।
जीवः सर्वमलं ज्ञात्वा ज्ञाता द्रष्टेति मुह्यति ॥ २६ ॥

ātmano vikriyā nāsti buddherbodho na jātviti,
jīvaḥ sarvamalaṁ jñātvā jñātā draṣṭeti muhyati. (26)

आत्मनः – of the Self; विक्रिया – action; न – not; अस्ति – is; बुद्धेः – for the intellect; बोधः – capacity to experience; न – not; जातु – at all; इति – thus; जीवः – the individuality; सर्वमलं – everything; ज्ञात्वा – knowing; ज्ञाता – the knower; द्रष्टा – the seer; इति – thus; मुह्यति – deludes

26. *Ātman never does anything and the intellect of its own accord has no capacity to experience 'I know'. But the individuality in us due to delusion thinks that it itself is the seer and the knower.*

Human intellect by itself is not endowed with the powers of feeling, thinking, willing or wishing, because it is a product of matter which is inert and insentient. A bulb in itself has no light without it being wedded to the electric current.

Ātman is Knowledge itself and it is not affected by the mental thoughts and physical actions. The individuality (jīva), which is a reflection of the pure Consciousness in the mind, falsely identifies itself with the body-mind-intellect equipment due to ignorance (avidyā) of its true nature, and therefore, it comes to superimpose the characteristics of the true Self on these insentient matter envelopments. In this way the delusion that one is a seer, knower and so on, arises in the ego, all because of a false notion in it.

The substratum for all these changing phenomena is that changeless Ātman. This world of plurality with different names and forms seems to rise and fall like waves on the ocean. It is an illusion experienced upon that substratum (adhiṣṭhāna) painted by the fancy of the confused ego. Just as the waves are in and of the ocean only and they do not stand even for a moment apart from the oceanic water, so also the entire waves of creation are in and of that supreme substratum – they have no separate existence in themselves. This supreme substratum is the Ātman which stands ever unaffected in the least by the changes caused in the arena of time, space and causality.

The illumining Consciousness, because of which there is an awareness of the various objects and activities of the inner mind, is that supreme Reality. Thus, though waves after waves of sorrow, dejection, despair, joy, success, anger, jealousy or passion may come in his mind, he who knows the 'Knower' of these waves is not affected by them. Why should the sun dim because of the tragedies he is illumining or glow brighter when he is illumining a joyous scene? 'This Self I am, I am illumining my mental conditions. I know I am happy or unhappy, but these are the mental waves that I am illumining. I am the light of Consciousness. None of the conditions of the mind is me', this is the constant wisdom of the wise man.

Verse 27

रज्जुसर्पवदात्मानं जीवं ज्ञात्वा भयं वहेत्।
नाहं जीवः परात्मेति ज्ञातश्चेन्निर्भयो भवेत्॥ २७ ॥

rajjusarpavadātmānaṁ jīvaṁ jñātvā bhayaṁ vahet,
nāhaṁ jīvaḥ parātmeti jñātaścennirbhayo bhavet. (27)

रज्जुसर्पवत् – like a serpent in a rope; आत्मानं – oneself; जीवं – as the ego; ज्ञात्वा – considering; भयं – fear; वहेत् – is overcome by; न – not; अहं – I; जीवः – the individuality or the ego; परात्मा – the supreme Self; इति – thus; ज्ञातः – having understood; चेत् – if; निर्भयः – fearless; भवेत् – becomes

27. *Just as the person who regards a rope as a snake is overcome by fear, so also one considering oneself as the ego (jīva) is overcome by fear. The egocentric individuality in us becomes fearless by realising that it is not a jīva but the supreme Self.*

The superimposition of a snake on a rope takes place only when the existence of the rope is not perceived. Just as the vision of the snake gives us perceptions of the details of the snake, the pain of its bite and the fear of death that will be caused by the appearance of snake in place of the rope, so too, once a misapprehension starts, in its own imaginations it multiplies into a thousand baseless notions and the individual under his own delusions suffers the consequences thereof.

In the non-apprehension of the Self, the misapprehension of the gross body, mind and so on, are perceived as real and in this misunderstanding the confused ego is born to suffer its own illusory sorrows. We are not limited individuals as we take ourselves to be. There is a limitless region of experiences, beyond what is known at present and this is shut out from us because of our self-centred existence. When the realisation of the true nature of the Self comes to one – even as mere theoretical knowledge – he who was till then in a perpetual state of fear and sorrow, seems to wake up from his own limited existence and rediscovers himself to be the blissful Self which is all-pervading and eternal.

Verse 28

आत्मावभासयत्येको बुद्ध्यादीनीन्द्रियाण्यपि ।
दीपो घटादिवत्स्वात्मा जडैस्तैर्नावभास्यते ॥ २८ ॥

ātmāvabhāsayatyeko buddhyādīnīndriyāṇyapi,
dīpo ghaṭādivatsvātmā jaḍaistairnāvabhāsyate. (28)

आत्मा – the Self; अवभासयति – illumines; एकः – single; बुद्ध्यादीनि – intellect and so on; इन्द्रियाणि – sense organs; अपि – also; दीपः – lamp; घटादिवत् – like the pots and so on; स्वात्मा – itself; जडैः – inert; तैः – by themselves; न – not; अवभास्यते – illumined

28. *Just as a lamp illumines a jar or a pot, so also the Ātman illumines the mind, the sense organs and so on. These material objects cannot illumine themselves by themselves because they are inert.*

The street lamp is a silent, unperturbed witness of all that happens under its light. Whether it is a marriage procession or a funeral march, the light, unmoved by the feeling of joy or sorrow, sheds its glow on all those that come under it. The postman, unconcerned with the nature and contents of the communication, delivers to the addressee.

In fact, we ourselves are unconcerned with the different experiences of a co-passenger when we get into a train or bus. We never consider his loss or gain as our own, although we may sympathise with his loss and help him, the sorrow is only illumined by us.

The Self in us is the one illuminating factor, the pure Awareness, which alone illumines both the good and the bad in us at all times. The Self is that power on account of which the physical activities, the mental yearning and the intellectual throbbing become vivid and living for us. The Upaniṣad says, 'That which the mind cannot comprehend but what makes the mind cognise, know that to be Brahman and not that which people worship[1]. The matter combinations may vary in their endless variety, in their strength, vitality and energy but the one Spirit, which is changeless in all these varied manifestations of matter, is the one and only glory which gives the glitter of a show to the entire 'jagat' – a lively show indeed!

---

[1] *Kenopaniṣad*-1.5

Verse 29

स्वबोधे नान्यबोधेच्छा बोधरूपतयात्मनः ।
न दीपस्यान्यदीपेच्छा यथा स्वात्मप्रकाशने ॥ २९ ॥

svabodhe nānyabodhecchā bodharūpatayātmanaḥ,
na dīpasyānyadīpecchā yathā svātmaprakāśane. (29)

स्वबोधे – with reference to Self-knowledge; न – not; अन्यबोधेच्छा – need for other knowledge; बोधरूपतया – because Its form is Knowledge itself; आत्मनः – one's own; न – not; दीपस्य – for a lamp; अन्यदीपेच्छा – need for another lamp; यथा – just as; स्वात्मप्रकाशने – to illumine itself

29. *A lighted lamp does not need another lamp to illumine its light. So too, Ātman which is Knowledge itself, needs no other knowledge to know Itself.*

Light is necessary to see the furniture in a dark room of a house but to see the very light which illumines the furniture, do we require any other light? We do not call for the aid of any other light to see the very sun that illumines all the objects in the world, because the sun is of the nature of illumination. To understand, realise and experience the Self, the illumining light in all our experiences, in fact, in all beings at all times, no other light is necessary. Because, this Self alone is Real and this Self alone lights up the knowledge of the entire creation – known and unknown. This Self is the all Awareness, Consciousness Absolute.

If we remove the furniture and so on, from the presence of the light, the light does not cease to exist. Similarly, even if all the objects in this world – all our experiences in the waking, dream and deep sleep states – have ended, even then, the Awareness shall keep on shining as ever before, because the Ātman is eternal and self effulgent. To know this source of all lights, no other light is necessary.

The outer world of objects is illumined as long as I am extrovert. The moment I turn introvert and my attention is inward, I realise that, That light alone is the Real one which illumines the entire experiences everywhere, not only in my own heart but in the entire world of beings. Whatever be the technique we adopt, we are bound to realise this Reality if we faithfully follow the path laid down by the learned sages and experienced seers.

The intellect cannot comprehend the one homogeneous whole, because It is not an object of cognition. With a telescope I cannot see myself. I can only see other objects in front of me and around me. Similarly, so long as the intellect is there, it is indeed very useful to discriminate, to reason out, to analyse and to understand the objects and happenings in a field other than the intellect itself. Now, when we try to understand the transcendental Truth with that limited intellect in an objective fashion, the intellect is trying to achieve the impossible, for, the Self is ever the subject that illumines the very intellect that tries to understand the Self.

The gross body is an object of experience. The subtle mind is something separate from and subtler than this gross equipment. The intellect is still subtler and yet, even this is an object experienced by us. When we thus move more and more into the inward chambers in ourselves, we almost reach the subtlest of the thought existence, the intellectual field for the play of our ideas and ideologies, such as 'I know', 'I understand' and so on. When these thought waves die down, when there is nothing for the Consciousness to illumine, at that rare and sacred moment, the pure Consciousness alone remains illumining Itself, as a silent street lamp at midnight stands illumining itself.

In terms of the familiar analogy of the dream, the dreamer is none other than the waker, because when the dreamer wakes up from his dream, he rediscovers himself to be the waker; so too, in the supreme plane of Self-awareness and bliss when all duality has ended, when I remain in my own real nature, to understand, realise and experience that bliss of the Self (svarūpānanda), no other illumination is necessary. It is a question of one awakening oneself to the state of God-consciousness – the Selfhood.

Verse 30

निषिध्य निखिलोपाधीन्नेति नेतीति वाक्यतः ।
विद्यादैक्यं महावाक्यैर्जीवात्मपरमात्मनोः ॥ ३० ॥

niṣidhya nikhilopādhīnneti netīti vākyataḥ,
vidyādaikyaṁ mahāvākyairjīvātmaparamātmanoḥ. (30)

निषिध्य – after negating; निखिलोपाधीन् – all conditionings; न इति – as not this; न इति – as not this; इति – thus; वाक्यतः – from the scriptural statements (commandments); विद्यात् – know; ऐक्यं – oneness; महावाक्यैः – by the great mahāvākyas; जीवात्मपरमात्मनः – of the individual soul and the supreme soul

30. *By the process of negation of the conditionings (upādhis) as per the scriptural statement 'It is not this, It is not this', the oneness of the individual soul and the supreme soul as indicated by the great mahāvākyas has to be realised.*

The Vaidika aphorisms (mahāvākyas) are – (1) tat tvam asi – That thou art, (2) ayam ātmā brahma – This Ātman is Brahman, (3) prajñānam brahma – Consciousness is Brahman, (4) ahaṁ brahma asmi – I am Brahman. All these point out the non-dual identity between the individual soul (jīva) and the supreme soul (Ātman) since the Reality behind both of them is the non-dual Brahman, the Absolute.

Self-realisation is attained by the negation of the upādhis or limiting factors of the Self, which are the gross, subtle and causal bodies and the inert objects of the outer world perceived through these matter equipments. This verse describes the above process and thus leads a seeker to realise the ultimate Truth that the individual soul (jīvātman) in its own true nature is nothing but the supreme Self (Paramātman).

The pure Consciousness in me is the absolute Reality and this alone, which is in you and in every other being, is the Self everywhere. The Guru declares this Truth as the very Self of the seeker 'That thou art'. The seeker of Truth in his burning aspirations to reach the goal, analyses his own matter vestures (upādhis) and also their corresponding objects in the outer world; the body and the sense objects, the mind and its feelings, and the intellect and its thoughts. With his powers of discrimination, he rejects everyone of them as the not-Self. Time, space and causality are also negated as perceptions of the mind and intellect. In this process of negation as 'not this', 'not this' (neti neti), when one has ascertained that the Self is not any of the not-Self vestures 'within' or the perceptions of mind-intellect 'without', then for a person of true wisdom, realisation of the one eternal Truth that persists in every object as the only permanent in the impermanent[1], becomes a living experience.

The mahāvākyas are no mere aphorisms but they are the golden keys which open the gateways to a richer experience which is beyond words and equally beyond the comprehension by our intellect. By a process of negation of the false and the assertion of the positive Truth, one reaches

---

[1] *Kaṭhopaniṣad*-2.5.13

the holy land of ultimate spiritual experience – I am Brahman (ahaṁ brahmāsmi).

That in all the mahāvākyas there is an implied suggestion of plurality is a criticism that we generally hear, raised by the dvaitins against the Śaṅkara's philosophy. According to the dualist, the very mahāvākya – 'That thou art' – implies two different objects in its two distinct pronouns. 'That' meaning the unknown goal to be realised and 'thou' meaning the seeker, and therefore, there are two aspects, the seeker and the sought, each having a distinctly separate existence. Two different things cannot be one and the same; therefore, at best a seeker can only keep a relative relationship with the ideal and can never hope to gain oneness with and be the perfection.

Ācārya Śaṅkara meets this controversy by indicating that even in the ordinary conversation we often employ this sort of a superficially dualistic declaration to indicate the essential non-dual factor. Let us take the sentence – 'This is that Gupta'. Herein, although two pronouns are used as 'this' and 'that', they indicate one and the same Mr. Gupta. The difference is only in the conditionings around Mr. Gupta. When it said 'That Mr. Gupta whom you met at Banārasa in 1950 as a petty shopkeeper, is this Mr. Gupta now we meet in Delhi in 1960 as a multimillionaire'. The conditioning factors around Mr. Gupta then and now are certainly different. Banārasa is not Delhi, 1950 is not 1960, a petty shopkeeper is not a multimillionaire. But when the conditionings are removed, the individual whom we met at Banārasa in the past under certain conditions is the very same individual whom we are meeting today in a different period of time and place and under different conditions.

Similarly, this jīva conditioned by the body, mind and intellect, bound by its own vāsanās, tempted by an endless array of objects, going through a thousand sorrows and despairs, is the same as the unconditioned, infinite, immutable Truth (Saccidānanda). The jīva in its limitations and sorrows can never be all-blissful, unlimited Brahman; however, when the jīva dissociates itself from all its matter embellishments, the jīva gets relieved from its egocentric individuality and comes to experience the Truth Divine.

The term 'asi' indicates this common denominator in both the jīva and the Īśvara. The Infinite conditioned by matter is the jīva. Having transcended its equipments, the jīva comes to rediscover itself to be nothing other than the immaculate Divine.

Verse 31

आविद्यकं शरीरादि दृश्यं बुद्बुदवत्क्षरम्
एतद्विलक्षणं विद्यादहं ब्रह्मेति निर्मलम्॥ ३१॥

āvidyakaṁ śarīrādi dṛśyaṁ budbudavatkṣaram,
etadvilakṣaṇaṁ vidyādahaṁ brahmeti nirmalam. (31)

आविद्यकं – upto the causal body; शरीरादि – body and so on; दृश्यं – perceived objects; बुद्बुदवत् – as bubbles; क्षरम् – perishable; एतद्विलक्षणं – different from all these; विद्यात् – realise; अहं – I; ब्रह्म – Brahman; इति – thus; निर्मलम् – pure

31. *The body and so on, upto the causal body (ignorance) are objects perceived and thus they are as perishable as bubbles. Realise through discrimination that I am ever the pure Brahman entirely different from all these.*

The five layers of matter explained earlier are all vehicles for the expression of life. The gross, subtle and causal bodies are all conditionings through which the Consciousness – through a process of identification[1] – expresses Itself as an experiencer in the different planes of consciousness.[2] The Self, identifying with the gross body becomes the waker

[1] To live and act as 'I am the body' is our body identification. During an identification, the subject forgets his own real nature and projects upon himself the nature of some other person or thing and hence, suffers or enjoys its sorrows and joys.

[2] The waking state, the dream state and the dreamless deep sleep state are known as the three planes of consciousness.

who experiences the waking state, and the same Self when it shifts Its identifications entirely to the subtle body becomes the dreamer. The dreamer lives his dreams and gathers his experiences of the dreamworld's multiplicity. When the Self, which has thus played the part of the waker and the dreamer, withdraws Itself and identifies with the causal body, It again acquires the attitude of the sleeper and comes to enjoy the total negation of the multiple experiences enjoyed or suffered during the earlier planes of consciousness, namely, the waking and the dream.

Identifying with the gross, subtle and causal bodies, if the Self becomes the waker, the dreamer and the deep sleeper respectively, then the Self in Itself must be something other than Its manifestations in these three states. The verse under discussion asserts this very fact, and the seekers are asked to rediscover the Self which is other than the perishable matter envelopments, through a close subjective Realisation.

It is only through discrimination that I must undo the evil and realise that which is perceived or brought within the field of my perceptions, feelings and comprehensions, must be different from the perceiver (sense organs), the feeler (mind) and the comprehending faculty (intellect). The divine Spark within me is the one illuminator which illumines each and everyone of these objects. Things illumined are always different from the illuminator. Thus the objects recognised by me are certainly different from the pure Self within me, the eternal subject.

Verse 32

देहान्यत्वान्न मे जन्मजराकार्श्यलयादयः ।
शब्दादिविषयैः सङ्गो निरिन्द्रियतया न च ॥ ३२ ॥

dehānyatvānna me janmajarākārśyalayādayaḥ,
śabdādiviṣayaiḥ saṅgo nirindriyatayā na ca. (32)

देहान्यत्वात् – because I am other than the body; न – not; मे – for me; जन्मजराकार्श्यलयादयः – birth, wrinkling, senility, death and so on; शब्दादिविषयैः – with sense objects such as sound and so on; सङ्गः – association; निरिन्द्रियतया – because I am without the sense organs; न – not; च – and

32. *I am other than the body, and so I am free from the changes such as birth, wrinkling, senility, death and so on. I have nothing to do with the sense objects such as sound and taste, for I am without the sense organs.*

The idea of an eternal substratum for the entire multiple world has been already established. Now, in the following six verses the process of negation of the body, mind and intellect are given, so that we may ultimately experience the Self as the sole illuminator of all objects.

If I am not the body, the merciless destinies through which it is being dragged are also not mine. The endless changes that come to me – birth, growth, decay, disease and death – in my pilgrimage from birth to death, all belong to the physical body, because I, the Self, is unborn. When there is no birth for me, there can be no death either, and therefore, no other changes such as growth, senility and so on, can ever come to me. If I mistake any of these to be mine, it is unfortunately the tragic error of the limited ego in me, suffering from the body-consciousness.

Being other than the body, I am unattached to the sense objects as well. If I am not the physical body or the sense organs, what am I then? A zero? A non-entity?

I am the Consciousness which illumines all the inert world of matter in and around me. I am the absolute immutable Spirit that revels everywhere and yet remains ever unattached.

Verse 33

अमनस्त्वान्न मे दुःखरागद्वेषभयादयः ।
अप्राणो ह्यमनाः शुभ्र इत्यादिश्रुतिशासनात् ॥ ३३ ॥

amanastvānna me duḥkharāgadveṣabhayādayaḥ,
aprāṇo hyamanāḥ śubhra ityādiśrutiśāsanāt. (33)

अमनस्त्वात् – because of not being the mind; न – not; मे – for me; दुःखरागद्वेषभयादयः – sorrow, attachment, malice, fear and so on; अप्राणः – without prāṇa; हि – verily; अमनाः – without mind; शुभ्रः – pure; इत्यादिश्रुतिशासनात् – and so on, for the scriptures declare

33. *I am other than the mind and hence, I am free from sorrow, attachment, malice and fear, for 'The Self is without prāṇa and without mind, pure and so on', is the commandment of the great scripture, the Upaniṣads.*

The mind is that substantial hallucination of terrific force and irresistible might that we feel in ourselves when our thoughts flow. It is ever-changing in its contents and in its moods. Without a 'thought flow' (mind) man does not exist as man even for a moment. All the same, I am not the mind, although I have a mind. My real nature is the Self, the changeless and the eternal. The idiosyncrasies of the mind are its own creation. The mind flourishes on thoughts and thoughts gurgle from my own desires acquired from my perception and experience of objects extraneous to myself.

Thus when I am really something other than the mind, and when I realise that it is the illumination of the Self that gives the power of awareness to this inert matter, the mind, I cannot but remain totally unaffected by the eruptions in that aspect of my physical structure. When I have awakened from my dream, I can no longer mourn for the dream child that died in my dream. I cease to identify myself with the mental emotions and so how can I any longer be a victim of the onslaught of sorrow, fear and so on, which are but the modifications of my mind? I am without a mind, I am pure Intelligence itself. I am that higher and imperishable Truth which is beyond all explanation and beyond the concept of time but within the experience of everyone when there is Self-realisation.

Even Ācārya Śaṅkara must not dogmatically assert without reference to the scriptures. Hence he quotes his authority – the Upaniṣads.

Verse 34

निर्गुणो निष्क्रियो नित्यो निर्विकल्पो निरञ्जनः ।
निर्विकारो निराकारो नित्यमुक्तोऽस्मि निर्मलः ॥ ३४ ॥

nirguṇo niṣkriyo nityo nirvikalpo nirañjanaḥ,
nirvikāro nirākāro nityamukto'smi nirmalaḥ. (34)

निर्गुणः – without attributes; निष्क्रियः – without actions; नित्यः – eternal; निर्विकल्पः – without any desire and thought; निरञ्जनः – without any dirt; निर्विकारः – without any change; निराकारः – without form; नित्यमुक्तः – ever liberated; अस्मि – I am; निर्मलः – ever pure

34. *I am attributeless, actionless, eternal, formless, without any desire, thought or modification, ever liberated and ever pure.*

A substance is that which has both physical and chemical properties (guṇas). All substances are matter. In this verse it is stated that I (Self) am without any properties (nirguṇa); thereby making it very clear that I am something other than matter. Matter has properties and it is finite. The Self has no properties, therefore, It is eternal. Desires and thoughts arise from the mind-intellect equipment and naturally, the Self, which is the Truth transcending these two, has none of these characteristic features. By these two preceding terms 'nitya' and 'nirvikalpa', the gross and sublte body are negated respectively, in the Ātman. So too, the causal body[1]

[1] The total vāsanās constituting avidyā is the causal body.

is negated by the next term 'nirañjanaḥ' or dirtless, meaning bereft of all vāsanās – immaculate.

Such a Truth having all the above four aspects must be one without any change and also without form. Naturally, It must be ever liberated and ever pure.

When I have negated all the superimposed limitations, the one substratum on which hangs the entire world of matter, the one Awareness 'asmi' (Is-ness) which illumines all thoughts, stands all by Itself gloriously alone. Then I rediscover myself to be that immutable Self which is changeless in the changing phenomena, like the gold in the ornaments or the clay in the pots. That real Self of mine is formless, ever liberated, eternal, pure and without attributes or actions.

Verse 35

अहमाकाशवत्सर्वं बहिरन्तर्गतोऽच्युतः ।
सदा सर्वसमः शुद्धो निःसङ्गो निर्मलोऽचलः ॥ ३५ ॥

ahamākāśavatsarvaṁ bahirantargato'cyutaḥ,
sadā sarvasamaḥ śuddho niḥsaṅgo nirmalo'calaḥ. (35)

अहम् – I; आकाशवत् – like space; सर्वम् – all things; बहिः – without; अन्तर्गतः – within; अच्युतः – changeless; सदा – always; सर्वसमः – same in all; शुद्धः – pure; निस्सङ्गो – unattached; निर्मलः – stainless; अचलः – motionless

35. *Like the space I fill all things within and without. Changeless and the same in all, at all times, I am pure, unattached, stainless and motionless.*

This verse also asserts the true nature of the Self. Space fills up all things in this world, and even that seemingly endless element of infinite expanse is a mere concept of the mind. That which is beyond time, space and causality is the Self in me and this cannot be localised at any given point in this body. Also, space (ākāśa) allows everything to exist in it, but itself never gets contaminated by the things which find their accommodation and existence in it. So too, the Self, though It allows the perceptions of the not-Self in It, is not contaminated by them.

The Self is one, eternal, immutable and It is the same in all. Also, It is equally divine in all beings. I am the pure Self, uncontaminated by the layers of matter around me, unattached, ever stainless, I am that all-pervading Brahman.

Verse 36

नित्यशुद्धविमुक्तैकमखण्डानन्दमद्वयम् ।
सत्यं ज्ञानमनन्तं यत्परं ब्रह्माहमेव तत् ॥ ३६ ॥

nityaśuddhavimuktaikamakhaṇḍānandamadvayam,
satyaṁ jñānamanantaṁ yatparaṁ brahmāhameva tat. (36)

नित्यशुद्धविमुक्तैकम् – eternal, pure, ever liberated, one; अखण्डानन्दम् – indivisible homogeneous bliss; अद्वयम् – non-dual; सत्यं – Existence; ज्ञानम् – Knowledge; अनन्तं – Infinite, यत् परं ब्रह्म – that supreme Brahman; अहम् एव – I alone; तत् – that

36. *I am verily that supreme Brahman which is eternal, pure, ever liberated, one, indivisible, blissful, non-dual Truth and of the nature of Existence-Knowledge-Infinite.*

We all have to gain a personal experience of the Self, therefore, the nature of our true Self is reiterated by Ācārya Śaṅkara. We need these verses for the purpose of meditation. Being constantly aware of the true nature of the Self is practice of knowledge (jñāna-abhyāsa). To contemplate over them and to feel them sincerely is the direct path to experience the Self.

Only those who constantly practise the control of the mind and retreat inch by inch from the dark despairs of the matter envelopments, can grow more and more in their spiritual strength. This brings the glow of the God-consciousness deep into their hearts and when the ignorance

– which causes the veiling of Truth and the agitations of the mind – has gradually weakened and when there is no more eruption of the self-centred egoistic thoughts of passions and sense impulses, we are awakened to the knowledge of the Self. This glory in us is ever pure, eternal and indivisible as previously stated and this is the supreme Existence-Knowledge-Infinite (satyam-jñānam-anantam).

Verse 37

एवं निरन्तराभ्यस्ता ब्रह्मैवास्मीति वासना ।
हरत्यविद्याविक्षेपान्रोगानिव रसायनम् ॥ ३७ ॥

evaṁ nirantarābhyastā brahmaivāsmīti vāsanā,
haratyavidyāvikṣepānrogāniva rasāyanam. (37)

एवम् – thus; निरन्तराभ्यस्ता – practised constantly; ब्रह्म एव अस्मि – I am Brahman; इति – thus; वासना – impression; हरति – destroys; अविद्याविक्षेपान् – ignorance and agitations; रोगान् – diseases; इव – like; रसायनम् – medicine

37. *The impression 'I am Brahman' thus created by constant practice destroys ignorance and the agitations caused by it, just as medicine or rasāyana destroys diseases.*

The knowledge of the identity of Brahman and Ātman stated above, when intensified by long reflection, destroys ignorance just as medicine administered cures the diseases and itself gets eliminated.

Constant practice is emphasised because over a period of past lives, a lot of vāsanās have accumulated and we have to get rid of them; also we must eliminate all our attachments and identifications with our body-mind-intellect equipment. The seeker of Truth should ever remember the detached nature of the pure Self and thus come to give up all his identifications with his material sheaths, and therefore, all his egocentric misconceptions about himself.

It is the ego that takes an individual (jīva) again and again to bondage and it is the ego again that keeps him bound to the world of ignorance. When the duality is removed then even the thought, 'I am Brahman', is dissolved in the all-consuming knowledge of the Self. There remains but one all-absorbing experience of the non-dual, eternal and infinite supreme Self. This subjective experience alone is the final culmination of all spiritual seeking because the Self is not an object of cognition. It is the very light which illumines all our experiences.

So, by constant 'jñāna-abhyāsa' we have to eliminate all the vāsanās, end the mind and come to experience that Self which is our essential nature. Just as the medicine we take in, of its own accord gets ultimately eliminated from us, so too the experience 'I am Brahman' is also dissolved in that spiritual glow[1]. So long as we are not asleep we try to sleep but when we reach sleep all efforts end by themselves.

1 *Ātmabodha*-5. In place of 'I am the body' idea, in case the seeker maintains the constant remembrance that 'I am Brahman', it will create a new set of divine vāsanās, which will act as an antidote to the egocentric vāsanās. The sense of individuality (jīva-bhāvanā) brings about more and more agitations, while spiritual vāsanās (Brahma vāsanās) quieten the thought flow. This process will continue until the last of the thoughts end and in the supreme silence of the mind, the Brahma vāsanā also ends – leaving the seeker to experience the Self.

Verse 38

विविक्तदेश आसीनो विरागो विजितेन्द्रियः ।
भावयेदेकमात्मानं तमनन्तमनन्यधीः ॥ ३८ ॥

viviktadeśa āsīno virāgo vijitendriyaḥ,
bhāvayedekamātmānaṁ tamanantamananyadhīḥ. (38)

विविक्तदेश – in a solitary place; आसीनः – seated; विरागः – free from desires; विजितेन्द्रियः – controlling the senses; भावयेत् – meditate upon; एकम् – one; आत्मानं – the Self; तम् – that; अनन्तम् – boundless; अनन्यधीः – with unswerving attention

38. *Sitting in a solitary place, freeing the mind from desires and controlling the senses, meditate upon the Ātman which is one without a second, with unswerving attention.*

This verse explains the path of meditation, which takes you face to face with the Reality. Sitting in a lonely place with no disturbances around you, no agitations of the mind or any wild roamings of the intellect, leaving behind all mental emotions and intellectual thoughts – which generally make the corner you sit, noisy with your thundering desires and roaring expectations – and with the sense organs (indriyas) now brought perfectly under your own control, identify with the Self indicated above, as your own nature – this is meditation. Meditate without any other thought in your mind, in that quiet and sequestered atmosphere. Meditate upon that infinite Ātman which is one without a second.

Be bold to assert the holy idea – in that lonely intellectual field, which transcends the concept of time – that you are that very same supreme Being which is all-pervading, pure and eternal. This self transformation is known as bhāvanā[1].

[1] It is very difficult to find an appropriate word in English for the Sanskrit term 'bhāvanā'. It is not a mere intellectual appreciation, nor is it a mere emotional wooing. And yet it is both. When both (the function of intellect, thinking and the function of the mind, feeling) are harmoniously woven together we get the 'heart' and its function is the bhāvanā. The ardent courtings of the mind and the intellect end in their marriage at the altar of heart and the joy of this nuptial is bhāvanā.

Verse 39

आत्मन्येवाखिलं दृश्यं प्रविलाप्य धिया सुधीः ।
भावयेदेकमात्मानं निर्मलाकाशवत्सदा ॥ ३९ ॥

ātmanyevākhilaṁ dṛśyaṁ pravilāpya dhiyā sudhīḥ,
bhāvayedekamātmānaṁ nirmalākāśavatsadā. (39)

आत्मनि एव – in the Ātman alone; अखिलं – entire; दृश्यं – world of objects; प्रविलाप्य – merging; धिया – by the intellect; सुधीः – wise man; भावयेत् – should think; एकम् – one; आत्मानं – the Self; निर्मलाकाशवत् – like the stainless or pure space; सदा – constantly

39. *The wise one should intelligently merge the entire world of objects in the Ātman alone and constantly think of the Self as being ever uncontaminated like space.*

Intelligent discrimination is the secret of a seeker's success in discovering Truth. When he has realised the supremacy of the Self, does the outer world exist for him? If not, why is it so? How does it happen?

The pure intellect, in its light of discrimination has brought forth the experience of Truth for the seeker. In that light of discrimination if we analyse and withdraw ourselves completely from the matter envelopments, we should thereafter have no more occasions to moan over the past, agitate at the present or worry for the future. There can be no wrong perceptions any more of the Truth for us.

When one crosses over the frontiers of the dream experiences, the entire dreamworld merges into one's own mind and the same dreamer now rediscovers himself to be the waker. The entire waking world merges back into the pure Awareness, from which it had risen. Now, all that remains is the pure non-dual Self. Just as the dreamworld has gone back and merged into the very waking mind that dreamt the dream, so too, the waking world of perceptions ends in the experience of the Ātman, the illuminator of all finite experiences.

Verse 40

रूपवर्णादिकं सर्वं विहाय परमार्थवित्।
परिपूर्णचिदानन्दस्वरूपेणावतिष्ठते ॥ ४० ॥

rūpavarṇādikaṁ sarvaṁ vihāya paramārthavit,
paripūrṇacidānandasvarūpeṇāvatiṣṭhate. (40)

रूपवर्णादिकं – form, colour and so on; सर्वं – everything; विहाय – discarding; परमार्थवित् – one who has realised the Supreme; परिपूर्णचिदानन्दस्वरूपेण अवतिष्ठते – remains as an embodiment of the infinite Consciousness and bliss

40. *He who has realised the Supreme, discards all his identifications with the objects of names and forms. Thereafter he dwells as an embodiment of the infinite Consciousness and bliss. He becomes the Self.*

The way to realise the Supreme and to be ever in the experience of the infinite Consciousness and bliss has already been explained – the only path is single pointed meditation. By constant practice of meditation, when one has gained the experience of the supreme Self (Paramārthavit), the illusory world of plurality, which was but a false superimposition upon the substratum, the Self, is no more.

When the world of names and forms merges into the substratum, the knower himself becomes the knower of the supreme Self, which is the embodiment of the infinite

Consciousness and bliss. To explain – the dreamer cannot see, experience or understand the waker, because upon waking the dreamer himself becomes the waker. No more are the dreams for him, for he has awakened to a brighter, clearer and ampler world of the waking state of consciousness. Just as the dreamer has ended his dream upon waking, so too, all the perceptions of the world recognised by the limited ego end when it realises the supreme state of pure Consciousness. The egocentric individual becomes the true Self, the Brahman.

Verse 41

ज्ञातृज्ञानज्ञेयभेदः परे नात्मनि विद्यते ।
चिदानन्दैकरूपत्वाद्दीप्यते स्वयमेव हि ॥ ४१ ॥

jñātṛjñānajñeyabhedaḥ pare nātmani vidyate,
cidānandaikarūpatvāddīpyate svayameva hi. (41)

ज्ञातृज्ञानज्ञेयभेदः – distinctions like knower, knowledge and the object of knowledge; परे – supreme; न – not; आत्मनि – in the Self; विद्यते – is; चिदानन्दैकरूपत्वात् – because It is of the nature of Consciousness and Bliss; दीप्यते – shines; स्वयम् एव – by Itself; हि – verily

41. *There are no distinctions such as, 'knower', 'knowledge' and 'the object of knowledge' in the supreme Self. Since It is of the nature of homogeneous Consciousness and Bliss, the Self has no such distinctions within Itself. It shines by Itself.*

The intellect is capable of perceiving only objects other than itself and so all our knowledge is constituted by the knowledge of things other than ourselves. An intelligent life in this world, in terms of our experiences of knowing things, is possible only by a contact of the experiencer with the objects of experience. A world of objects is as much necessary as the subject who is the experiencer and between the experiencer and the experienced a certain relationship should remain which is known as experiencing. Without these three fundamental factors – the subject, the object and the necessary relationship between the two, no experience is possible.

Being non-dual, homogeneous and eternal, the Self cannot suffer in Itself any distinction such as the subject or the object, and therefore, every seeker enquires, 'If it is so, with what instrument or equipment will I experience the Self when I have transcended the sense perceptions, mental feelings and intellectual thoughts?' Transcending these known equipments and their fields of objects, if there be the Truth, who will realise It, and by what instrument? The answer is that the Self is the very Consciousness by which all thoughts, feelings and perceptions are illumined and when all these are eliminated, to know Knowledge no other knowledge is necessary[1]. Self is Knowledge itself; It is Consciounsness Itself. When the furniture is removed from a room in the daytime, what happens to the sun? Whether there are objects or not, its illumination is unaffected, it illumines itself, and to see the sun no other light or torch is necessary.

[1] 'no other knowledge is necessary' – here the term 'knowledge' is used to mean instrument of knowing.

Verse 42

एवमात्मारणौ ध्यानमथने सततं कृते ।
उदितावगतिर्ज्वाला सर्वाज्ञानेन्धनं दहेत् ॥ ४२ ॥

evamātmāraṇau dhyānamathane satataṁ kṛte,
uditāvagatirjvālā sarvājñānendhanaṁ dahet. (42)

एवम् – thus; आत्मा – of the Self; अरणौ – in the araṇi (wooden piece); ध्यानमथने – churning in the form of contemplation; सततं – constantly; कृते – when done; उदिताअवगतिर्ज्वाला – fire of Knowledge that is born; सर्व अज्ञानेन्धनम् – all the fuel of ignorance; दहेत् – shall burn

42. *Thus, when the lower and the higher aspects of the Self are churned together, the fire of Knowledge which is generated shall burn down all the fuel of ignorance.*

Ignorance is destroyed only when there is constant churning of Knowledge – 'I am the Self and not this assemblage of mere body, sense organs, mind and intellect'. Constructive thoughts of this nature, when constantly nourished in meditation with single pointed devotion, right understanding and discrimination – described in this verse as 'dhyāna-mathana' or the churning in the form of contemplation – reveals the true nature of the Self as Bliss Absolute and puts an end to ignorance once and for all. The fire of Knowledge generated by this churning very soon becomes a mighty conflagration and all misconceptions due to ignorance are burnt down, just as the fire consumes all the fuel and burns it down.

The 'churning of knowledge' is elaborately described in the *Kaivalyopaniṣad*. In the ancient days, for the purpose of the rituals, fire was produced by churning a wooden rod on two wooden pieces hollowed out for the ends of the rod to rest. When the rod is churned in these sockets (araṇī) pressed down firmly, the friction creates heat and fire. This very idea is adopted in this beautiful metaphor. The lower ego and the higher Self are 'churned' with the mahāvākya, 'I am Brahman' (ahaṁ brahmāsmi). When this churning (dhyāna-mathana) is done properly, the fire of Knowledge is generated. Meditation fans it into a conflagration in which all our misconceptions and ignorance are burnt down[1].

[1] *Kaivalyopaniṣad*-11

Verse 43

अरुणेनेव बोधेन पूर्वं सन्तमसे हृते ।
तत आविर्भवेदात्मा स्वयमेवांशुमानिव ॥ ४३ ॥

aruṇeneva bodhena pūrvaṁ santamase hṛte,
tata āvirbhavedātmā svayamevāṁśumāniva. (43)

अरुणेन – by the Lord of the early dawn (aruṇa); इव – like; बोधेन – by the knowledge; पूर्वं सन्तमसे – the universal darkness that existed before; हृते – when dispelled; ततः – then, आविर्भवेत् – rises; आत्मा – the Self; स्वयम् एव – of Its own accord; अंशुमान् – the sun; इव – like

43. *Just as the sun rises soon after the Lord of the early dawn (aruṇa) has dispelled the thick darkness that existed before, so too, the Self manifests on Its own accord, once the right knowledge has dispelled ignorance.*

Ignorance is the thick pall of vāsanās. We have to break through this darkness before we can get into the lit up citadel of Truth, the treasure house of the Experience Divine.

Aruṇa, the dawn heralds the sun. Soon after the early dawn, a very short time after the east has glowed with the golden hue of the dawn (aruṇa) and thus dispelled the darkness of the night, we get the vision of the brilliant sun illumining the world. In the same way, when the egocentric existence in us, that obstructs the vision of the Self, is falsified by constant and diligent meditation, the vision of the true Self arises in all Its glory.

The vision of the Self is obstructed by none other than our own mental agitations and egocentric vanities. Meditation quietens the thought flow and consequently the mind's extrovertedness. When a mind, thus pacified and withdrawn from its outer activities, turns inward, it springs forth to drown itself in the experience of the Self and to become one with it.

Verse 44

आत्मा तु सततं प्राप्तोऽप्यप्राप्तवदविद्यया ।
तन्नाशे प्राप्तवद्भाति स्वकण्ठाभरणं यथा ॥ ४४ ॥

ātmā tu satataṁ prāpto'pyaprāptavadavidyayā,
tannāśe prāptavadbhāti svakaṇṭhābharaṇaṁ yathā. (44)

आत्मा – the Self; तु – verily; सततं – always; प्राप्तः – ever existing; अपि – yet; अप्राप्तवत् – as though not realised; अविद्यया – because of ignorance; तत् नाशे – when that (ignorance) is dispelled; प्राप्तवत् – like an object gained; भाति – appears; स्वकण्ठाभरणं – the ornament of one's neck; यथा – just as

44. *Ātman is an ever existing Reality. Yet, because of ignorance It is not realised. Therefore, as soon as the ignorance is dispelled, the Ātman is realised. It is like the missing ornament of one's neck.*

Knowledge lies veiled by ignorance, 'ajñānena āvṛtam jñānam.' No one can give a dreamer his experience as a waker. The dreamer himself is the waker. Similarly, there is no need to acquire or create a new personality in me to get into the higher realm of experience. I am ever the eternal, infinite bliss. However, if I am already not that and if I have to build up that new condition for me, then listening to, studying, reflecting upon and meditating on texts of Upaniṣads are the means prescribed. Yet we cannot say that because of these practices Ātman is 'created' – if the experience of the Self is due to the sādhanā, then, when sādhanā, the cause ends, then experience, the effect, must also end. What is created must die and end. The Infinite cannot be created as a result of the sādhanā. The Self is ever with us, however we recognise It only when the veil of ignorance is removed through constant and sincere sādhanā.

This Ātman is in all the states of experiences and in all beings and at all times. It is awake even while we are asleep, yet we are not aware of this eternal Self due to our preoccupations with the misapprehensions of the Reality. In fact, we live because of Its illuminations but we are blind to that Light Divine. When ignorance is removed, when we are out of the enveloping darkness, the cataract in the 'wisdom-eye' is cured, the glory of the Self is revealed – just as, when the clouds move away, the sun, whose light is already there, shines upon us.

When we have removed the veiling over the ever existent Self, we exclaim as though we have found out something which was not already there and this, however, is not the case. We were lamenting over something which we had never lost. We felt miserable over the loss of something which was actually not lost but on the other hand it was all along with us. Sometimes, we search for and get tired of our weary disappointments, when we cannot find our key which perhaps lies all the time in our own pocket. A lady can despair at the loss of a necklace, which is often still on her neck! We only rediscover the Self, which was all the time with us. When our ignorance of the Self ends through the discipline of meditation, we only rediscover It, which was all the time with us.

Verse 45

स्थाणौ पुरुषवद्भ्रान्त्या कृता ब्रह्मणि जीवता ।
जीवस्य तात्त्विके रूपे तस्मिन्दृष्टे निवर्तते ॥ ४५ ॥

sthāṇau puruṣavadbhrāntyā kṛtā brahmaṇi jīvatā,
jīvasya tāttvike rūpe tasmindṛṣṭe nivartate. (45)

स्थाणौ – in the post; पुरुषवत् – like the man; भ्रान्त्या – because of delusion; कृता – is made; ब्रह्मणि – in the Brahman; जीवता – individuality; जीवस्य – of the jīva; तात्त्विके रूपे – in the real nature; तस्मिन् – in the Self; दृष्टे – when seen; निवर्तते – is destroyed

45. *Just as a post appears to be a ghost, Brahman appears to be a jīva because of ignorance. The egocentric individuality is destroyed when the real nature of the jīva is realised as the Self.*

In delusion alone can we imagine and recognise a post to be a ghost. In fact, the misapprehension of the ghost has risen only from the non-apprehension of the post. Similarly, on the Brahman which is the supreme Self and the substratum for all, ignorance projects our egocentric existence and its world of diversity. In this confused state, we spin and weave for ourselves a cobweb of our own creation. Thereafter, we identify ourselves with our body, mind and intellect. Thus we get entirely caught up in a net of our own creation hatched from our own ignorance.

Just as the ghost disappears when the post is recognised, or just as the entire dreamworld rolls back into the very mind – from which it was projected – when the dreamer wakes up, so too, when we have come to experience the true Self in us, this illusory world that we have painted with all gay enchantment, also loses its reality once and for all.

The non-apprehension of the post has caused all the misapprehension as the head, trunk, limbs, dress, eyes, movements and so on, of the vivid vision of the ghost. The misconception was the ghost on the post. When the cause, the misconception ends, the effect, the ghost also disappears. When the ego-sense has ended, all its effects also end and there is no more any bondage suffered.

Verse 46

तत्त्वस्वरूपानुभवादुत्पन्नं ज्ञानमञ्जसा ।
अहं ममेति चाज्ञानं बाधते दिग्भ्रमादिवत् ॥ ४६ ॥

tattvasvarūpānubhavādutpannaṁ jñānamañjasā,
ahaṁ mameti cājñānaṁ bādhate digbhramādivat. (46)

तत्त्वस्वरूपानुभवात् – by experiencing the Truth; उत्पन्नं – produced; ज्ञानम् – knowledge; अञ्जसा – instantly; अहं – I; मम – mine; इति – thus; च – and; अज्ञानं – the ignorance; बाधते – destroys; दिग्भ्रमादिवत् – like the wrong notions about the directions

46. *Just as right information removes the wrong notion about the directions, so too, the knowledge that is gained as a result of the experience of the Truth, destroys the ignorance that is characterised by the notions of 'I-ness' and 'my-ness'.*

The Self-knowledge that is born out of the experience of the Reality immediately and instantaneously destroys ignorance (ajñāna) which has caused the wrong notions of the ego. This wrong conception of a limited, coloured and distorted personality has been the cause for the agency of actions and for the notions of 'I-ness' and 'my-ness' (sense of possession) in everyone.

When you feel confused about the directions in a new town, as to whether it is east or west, the sunrise helps you to locate the directions correctly. The limited ego-sense leads a confused life in the midst of the labyrinth of matter vestures and their perceptions, feeling and thoughts. But when the knowledge of the Truth dawns, one gains an understanding of the right way of living in and experiencing through the various matter equipments.

Śrī Śaṅkara seems to foresee here the possibility of a logical doubt in the mind of an intelligent student. Ordinarily in our intellectual life, knowledge of one object cannot remove the ignorance of other objects – for instance, knowledge of a pot cannot end the ignorance of the watch or the radio. Here, the verse seems to say that the knowledge arising out of the experience of the Self will remove the ignorance created concepts of 'I-ness' and 'my-ness'. Apparently this is a contradiction to our daily intellectual experience.

In order to elucidate this idea, Ācārya Śaṅkara has chosen a very appropriate illustration indeed. When a traveller is in confusion as to the direction in which he is moving, and on enquiry if some local person were to indicate to him the west, the knowledge arising out of this indication will instantly put an end to all his ignorance regarding the south, east and north. This is because, the other quarters have a definite relationship with the one known direction and with reference to that known direction, the traveller can, without any more help from the local man, know for himself the other three directions.

Similarly, when the Self is known, we shall immediately understand our true relationship with the world of objects around us and our own relationship with our matter envelopments. The sense of 'I' and the concept of 'mine' both become meaningless and delusory when the Self is realised as one universal Reality, ever the same, within and without.

The directions are ever there whether we know them or not. So long as we are confused, we take the east to be the west and so on. A right understanding gives us the true directions. So too, when Self is known we are able to fix our relationship in the world on surer footings, with more balanced vision.

Verse 47

सम्यग्विज्ञानवान्योगी स्वात्मन्येवाखिलं जगत्।
एकं च सर्वमात्मानमीक्षते ज्ञानचक्षुषा ॥ ४७ ॥

samyagvijñānavānyogī svātmanyevākhilaṁ jagat,
ekaṁ ca sarvamātmānamīkṣate jñānacakṣuṣā. (47)

सम्यक् – very well; विज्ञानवान् – Man of Realisation; योगी – the yogī; स्वात्मनि एव – in his own Self; अखिलं – entire; जगत् – universe; एकं – one; च – and; सर्वम् – everything; आत्मानम् – his own Self; ईक्षते – sees; ज्ञानचक्षुषा – through his eye of wisdom

47. The perfect yogī of Realisation and enlightenment sees, through his 'eye of wisdom' (jñāna-cakṣu), the entire universe in his own Self and regards everything else as his own Self and nothing else.

The yogī who has realised the true Self, who has been trained to integrate his mind and see the oneness of the Self everywhere, who has effaced his lower nature and learnt to live in harmony with the higher in him, whose mind and intellect are well controlled without their disturbing pull towards the outer world of objects – that Mahātman or Man of Wisdom sees the entire world as the manifestation of his own Self, and experiences the Self in him to be the Self everywhere.

He is convinced that there is no separate enlivening factor for the world outside, for the Self in him and for the different experiences in him. When the eye of Wisdom is opened, just as the oneness of gold is realised in all the ornaments, the supreme Reality alone is experienced to be all-pervading – within, without, here, there and everywhere.

When the ego which kept him in bondage – the 'jīvātman' which seemed to be labouring under limitations – is blasted to smithereens with the current of the Self-knowledge in him, he becomes a man of total and absolute fulfilment, the purpose of his life is achieved. The Truth of his existence is realised. The Reality in him is experienced.

Verse 48

आत्मैवेदं जगत्सर्वमात्मनोऽन्यन्न विद्यते ।
मृदो यद्वद्धटादीनि स्वात्मानं सर्वमीक्षते ॥ ४८ ॥

ātmaivedaṁ jagatsarvamātmano'nyanna vidyate,
mṛdo yadvadghaṭādīni svātmānaṁ sarvamīkṣate. (48)

आत्मा – the Ātman; एव – verily; इदं – this; जगत् – universe; सर्वम् – entire; आत्मनः अन्यत् – other than the Ātman; न – not; विद्यते – exists; मृदः – from clay; यद्वत् – in that manner; घटादीनि – pots and so on; स्वात्मानं – one's own Self; सर्वम् – everything; ईक्षते – sees

48. *The tangible universe is verily the Ātman Itself. Nothing whatsoever other than the Ātman exists. Just as pots and jars are verily made of clay and cannot be said to be anything but clay, so too, for the enlightened person, all that is perceived is the Self.*

In the earlier verses, it has been stated that the whole world of experience is nothing but the expression of one's own Self and there is nothing beyond this Supreme. How are we to accept this proposition that Ātman alone is the essence of the entire world of experiences?

Out of clay are made various kinds of pans and potteries. They come out of clay, exist in clay as clay and finally merge back to be known as the same old clay. Without clay, all the different shapes and forms could not have come about.

The original clay alone gave the shape and substantiality to the different existent pot units. Just as there is no separate existence for the clay pans and pots apart from the clay – just as the waves in the ocean are the same as the waters on which they have risen – so too, the Self alone is the Reality which has given shape and life to the world of names and forms, and this is rightly understood by the Man of Wisdom.

The ordinary folk, who have no greater purpose in life than to direct their energies towards a hunt for the fleeting pleasures of the world of objects, cannot so easily recognise this subtle presence everywhere. The Infinite pervades and envelops the entire finite world. The multiplicity is but a projection upon the one eternal infinite Truth.

Verse 49

जीवन्मुक्तस्तु तद्विद्वान्पूर्वोपाधिगुणांस्त्यजेत् ।
सच्चिदानन्दरूपत्वात् भवेत् भ्रमरकीटवत् ॥ ४९ ॥

jīvanmuktastu tadvidvānpūrvopādhiguṇāṁstyajet,
saccidānandarūapatvāt bhavet bhramarakīṭavat. (49)

जीवन्मुक्तः – liberated one; तु – verily; तत् विद्वान् – endowed with Self-knowledge; पूर्वोपाधिगुणान् – traits of the previous equipments; त्यजेत् – would give up; सच्चिदानन्दरूपत्वात् – because of nature of Existence-Consciousness-Bliss; भवेत् – will be; भ्रमरकीटवत् – like a wasp

49. *A liberated soul, endowed with Self-knowledge, gives up the traits of his previously explained equipments (upādhis), and because of his Sat-Cit-Ānanda nature, he verily becomes Brahman, as the worm transforming into the wasp.*

A liberated soul (Jīvanmukta) is one who has realised the infinitude of his existence and has become totally free from ignorance (avidyā) even while he lives in his body, which continues to exist as long as its prārabdha lasts. He who has so well integrated his spiritual personality as to totally renounce the properties of the matter envelopments and the ego; with his well directed, upright, physical, mental and intellectual activities, is an enlightened soul. He is one of the fortunate few who has died the 'mystic death' – the death of his limited individuality.

Such a Jīvanmukta who has lived the life of a spiritual giant, unshakeable in his inner experience and who has freed himself from all the attractions around him, lives verily as the divine Self. For him there is no question of any bondage from the earlier described gross, subtle and causal bodies (upādhis). He who is the knower of Brahman, becomes the Brahman which he was asserting all through his years of meditation, just as the worm becomes a wasp.

The wasp builds a clay nest with no other outlet but a small hole in it and places a worm in it. Now and then stinging the worm, the wasp keeps sitting at the door. The helpless worm, weary with fear and pain, constantly looks out at the terrible face of the wasp which is threatening to sting it again. The worm thus remaining in single pointed contemplation over the form and nature of the wasp, grows wings and totally metamorphoses to become a wasp itself.

Similarly, through the negation of matter and assertion of the Spirit, when the yogī for years meditates upon the divine nature of the Self, the egocentric limited individuality in him drops off its 'worm-existence' and becomes Existence itself, which is in fact our true Self, the Life Principle.

Verse 50

तीर्त्वा मोहार्णवं हत्वा रागद्वेषादिराक्षसान्।
योगी शान्तिसमायुक्तः आत्मारामो विराजते ॥ ५० ॥

tīrtvā mohārṇavaṁ hatvā rāgadveṣādirākṣasān,
yogī śāntisamāyuktaḥ ātmārāmo virājate. (50)

तीर्त्वा – after crossing; मोहार्णवं – the ocean of delusion; हत्वा – killing; रागद्वेषादिराक्षसान् – the monsters of likes and dislikes; योगी – the yogī; शान्तिसमायुक्तः – united with peace; आत्मारामः – one who revels within himself; विराजते – shines

50. *After crossing the ocean of delusion and killing the monsters of likes and dislikes, the yogī who is united with peace becomes Ātmārāma, that is, he comes to revel in himself.*

When the transformation is complete and the individualised, egocentric jīva has discovered its pure nature as the eternal Self, it crosses over all delusions (moha), which is non-apprehension or the causal body. The mental impressions gathered in his individualised existence all through his entire past, together constitute the ocean of delusion or ignorance. Through the process of meditation when the yogī reaches the effulgent experience of the Self, he has no doubt, crossed all non-apprehensions of Truth, and therefore, also all his misapprehensions about himself. This is possible only when the devilish forces of likes and dislikes are destroyed and eliminated within the individual seeker's heart.

Having crossed the ocean of delusion and destroyed all the monsters (rākṣasas) of negative tendencies, expressed by the mental equipment in an individualised self, the meditator enters the realm of the Self, to rediscover for himself the voiceless peace which he has but temporarily lost. Self is of the nature of Peace-Auspiciousness-Beauty (śāntam-śivam-sundaram). And this experience of the eternal Self is permanent and thus the meditator lives in himself, in an unbroken experience of endless peace and bliss. He is the one who revels in the Ātman (Ātmārāma).

This crucial word 'Ātmārāma', poetic in itself, is highly suggestive to a student of Upaniṣads and the Hindu classics. Śaṅkara, a Master of the Hindu traditions, brings the entire story of *Rāmāyaṇa* to pack up the words of this verse firmly into its mighty beauty. Sage Vālmīki who wrote *Rāmāyaṇa,* not only wanted to give his readers, a complete picture of an ideal human being facing every possible situation of life with utmost inner equipoise, but he also had his own experience of the Self to express. Vālmīki was not mere author and publisher. He was essentially a Man of Realisation, a champion of the scriptures. These inner symbolisms and significances of the *Rāmāyaṇa* are generally lost sight of by the students who are charmed away by the minute beauties in the workmanship of his pen. Śaṅkara in this verse hints at the deep significances of *Rāmāyaṇa* taken as a whole.

The very name of the hero of this great classic is significant and suggestive; Rāma means the one reveller who revels everywhere in all hearts – 'sarve ramanti iti rāmaḥ'. The Self, Rāma, wedded to Sītā, who is none other than

His own nature, peace, lives on joyously with unperturbed equanimity, both in the kingdom of Ayodhya and in the jungles of his exile. His sorrows start when his consort 'peace' falls prey into the hands of Rāvaṇa, the ten-headed monster. This represents the lower animal nature in an individual which has ten heads even today – the five organs of perception and the five organs of action. The kingdoms of the secular and of the materialist can never sustain for long within the boundaries of the Āryāvarta, the land of the Sanātana-dharma, the garden of spirituality. In an era of Rāmarājya, Rāvaṇas cannot be the governors.

Rāma then seeking his consort has to necessarily cross the ocean, reach Laṅkā, destroy the demoniac forces and rediscover Sītā, His lost peace. Śaṅkara mentions in this verse that the ocean to be bridged over is the delusory attachment and fascination, and the forces that array themselves against Rāma are the negative tendencies, which are natural in a deluded mind. When the inner personality is purified and rehabilitated, peace, the eternal consort of the Self, is regained. Thereafter, the Man of Realisation rules over the kingdom of life, from his capital known as 'Ayodhya'[1].

It is only in Sanskrit that a classic can be summarised by the suggestiveness of the words that are, at once, directly describing the highest spiritual Truth.

[1] The term 'Ayodhya' literally means without any war. Here it is used to indicate the state of effortlessness enjoyed by the Man of Realisation.

Verse 51

बाह्यानित्यसुखासक्तिं हित्वात्मसुखनिर्वृतः ।
घटस्थदीपवत्स्वस्थः स्वान्तरेव प्रकाशते ॥ ५१ ॥

bāhyānityasukhāsaktiṁ hitvātmasukhanirvṛtaḥ,
ghaṭasthadīpavatsvasthaḥ svāntareva prakāśate. (51)

बाह्यानित्यसुखासक्तिं – attachment for fleeting joys of the outer world; हित्वा – after having relinquished; आत्मसुखनिर्वृतः – contented with the bliss derived from the Self; घटस्थदीपवत् – like a lamp placed inside a jar; स्वस्थः – comfortably placed; स्वान्तः – within himself; एव – alone; प्रकाशते – shines

51. *The Self-abiding Jīvanmukta, relinquishing all his attachments to the fleeting joys of the outer world and satisfied with the bliss derived from the Ātman, shines inwardly like a lamp placed inside a jar.*

The goal of the seekers is no doubt the end of all sorrows and the achievement of perfect joy. He who has withdrawn his consciousness entirely from all his identifications with his body, mind and intellect, is known as a Man of Realisation. Naturally, therefore, he will not be conscious of the objects of these three layers of matter – namely, the world of sense objects, the variety of feelings and the array of ideas.

However, to the Self, in the Self, there is nothing but the Self to illumine. When the self effulgent Truth has nothing else other than Itself to illumine in Its own infinite glory, how will It exist? This will now be the doubt in the mind of every student of Vedānta, who is approaching the theory of Self-realisation; especially during his early days of study, when he is trying to appreciate philosophy through his own limited intellectual evaluations.

The condition of the pure Consciousness, when it has no other object to be conscious of except the Self, is beautifully brought out in this analogy by Śrī Śaṅkara. When a lighted lamp is put on a table, its glowing illumination plays upon the surfaces of the various objects in the room and in varying degrees of intensity it illumines the objects. But as soon as that lighted lamp is slowly and carefully lowered into a pot or a jar, the light of the lamp must come to illumine only the inner space of the jar. Similarly, Consciousness, while playing through the equipments no doubt gets reflected upon the objects and provides us with the knowledge of objects; but when we have withdrawn the Consciousness from the vehicles into Itself, It can illumine only Itself.

It is said in the verse that at this stage of meditation, 'The Self shines inwardly, all alone'. This should not be misunderstood to mean only the direct dictionary meaning of the term 'inward'. 'When the consciousness is withdrawn into the Self, It illumines the within' is a statement that is couched in the technical language of Vedānta. In Vedānta, subtlety of a thing is measured by its pervasiveness and the subtler is conceived as interior to the grosser. Naturally, therefore, the innermost Self, is the subtlest of the subtle – which means that It is all-pervading and nothing pervades It.

At the moment of Self-realisation – the final experience when the Consciousness comes to illumine 'within' – experience is that of the infinite, all-pervading, subtlest of the subtle, the ever effulgent Self of the nature of pure Awareness – this is the secret import of the verse under discussion.

Verse 52

उपाधिस्थोऽपि तद्धर्मैरलिप्तो व्योमवन्मुनिः ।
सर्वविन्मूढवत्तिष्ठेदसक्तो वायुवच्चरेत् ॥ ५२ ॥

upādhistho'pi taddharmairalipto vyomavanmuniḥ,
sarvavinmūḍhavattiṣṭhedasakto vāyuvaccaret. (52)

उपाधिस्थः अपि – though associated with conditionings; तद्धर्मैः – by their attributes; अलिप्तः – untainted; व्योमवत् – like the space; मुनिः – the contemplative one; सर्ववित् – one who knows everything; मूढवत् – like a fool; तिष्ठेत् – may remain; असक्तः – unattached; वायुवत् – like the wind; चरेत् – may move about

52. *Though he lives in the conditionings, just as the space, the contemplative one, may remain like a fool, ever unconcerned with anything or he may move about like the wind, totally unattached.*

In this verse, the state of a Jīvanmukta is described further. The perfect man is one who has renounced all his clinging attachments to the finite sense objects. The mind has a tendency to hold on to something or the other and what is the alternative offered here? It is the constant bliss in him.

But what happens when sometimes, he appears to be seemingly associated with the world? Even though he may be outwardly cognising and appearing to be aware of their existence, he is not bound by them, for, he is a free man now – free from conditionings (upādhis) of body, mind and intellect. As an illumined person, he has learnt to live constantly in that Knowledge, and the conditionings have no weight to pull him down.

He may move about like a devil, a child or as a drunken man but he is not really so. He lives in the greater intoxication of Godhood and in the subtler joy of Self-realisation. He may serve the society or he may not. All the same, put him in any situation, and he will handle it without getting affected in the least by his actions or the results of his contact. He is a 'sthitaprajña' of the highest order, explained so elaborately in the *Gītā*.[1]

The sky appears to be blue and a little grey but the sky itself is not really so. Similarly, the Jīvanmukta may seem to be associated with the upādhis and may wander as an ordinary man in the workaday world but he gets into that role and comes out of it unattached and untainted like the wind.

[1] *Holy Gītā*-2.54 to 72

Verse 53

उपाधिविलयाद्विष्णौ निर्विशेषं विशेन्मुनिः ।
जले जलं वियद्व्योम्नि तेजस्तेजसि वा यथा ॥ ५३ ॥

upādhivilayādviṣṇau nirviśeṣaṁ viśenmuniḥ,
jale jalaṁ viyadvyomni tejastejasi vā yathā. (53)

उपाधिविलयात् – on the dissolution of the upādhis or conditionings; विष्णौ – in the all-pervading Spirit; निर्विशेषं – attributeless; विशेत् – is absorbed; मुनिः – the contemplative one; जले – into water; जलं – water; वियत् – space; व्योम्नि – into space; तेजः – light; तेजसि – into light; वा – or; यथा – just as

53. *On the dissolution of the upādhis, the contemplative one, is totally absorbed in 'Viṣṇu', the all-pervading attributeless Spirit, like water into water, space into space or light into light.*

Identification with the upādhis of body, mind and intellect has occasioned the expression of my personality. No doubt, it may appear that there are other limiting factors, but all of them arise because of one's association with these three evils. The seeker who wants to end the conditioned existence and discover the whole in him, should withdraw his mind from the said 'upādhis'. When I no more identify myself with the individuality in me; when the egocentric existence, which is the Reality reflected in the mind and intellect, is sublated, then – like water into water, space into space or light into light, I come to merge with the Viṣṇu, the all-pervading.

Naturally, when my limited existence is made unlimited, I can be nothing else but the all-pervading. The stains on the mirror having been washed out, the reflection is now brighter and clearer.

When the equipments are sublated, the Muni, a man of reflection (mananaśīlavān), comes to experience the inner bliss without any admixture or qualitative distinction (nirviśeṣatvam). When the Viṣṇu or the all-pervasive nature of one's own Self is realised as the Self in all, one remains totally merged in Him (the true Self of one and all) in eternal joy, losing one's own limited individuality.

Verse 54

यल्लाभान्नापरो लाभो यत्सुखान्नापरं सुखम् ।
यज्ज्ञानान्नापरं ज्ञानं तद्ब्रह्मेत्यवधारयेत् ॥ ५४ ॥

yallābhānnāparo lābho yatsukhānnāparaṁ sukham,
yajjñānānnāparaṁ jñānaṁ tadbrahmetyavadhārayet. (54)

यत् लाभात् – apart from the attainment of which; न – no; अपरः – other; लाभः – attainment; यत् सुखात् – apart from the blessedness of which; न – no; अपरं – other; सुखम् – blessedness; यत् ज्ञानात् – apart from the knowledge of which; न – not; अपरं – other; ज्ञानं – knowledge; तत् ब्रह्म – that Brahman; इति – thus; अवधारयेत् – realise

54. *Realise that to be Brahman, the attainment of which leaves nothing more to be attained, the blessedness of which leaves no other blessing to be desired and the knowledge of which leaves nothing more to be known.*

The following three verses in *Ātmabodha* try to indicate the supreme Brahman through 'taṭastha lakṣaṇa'. For example, to indicate the house of Sat Prakashjī we may say, 'That house, on which the crow is perched, is his house'. The crow does not permanently sit there – the crow is not a part of that house. However, with the help of the crow we distinguish Sat Prakashjī's house from other similar houses. The house is of course, understood as the building without the crow on it. Even when the crow has flown away, one can recognise it amongst all other houses. This method of definition used in Vedānta is technically known as taṭastha lakṣaṇa.

The supreme experience is explained here as the greatest gain, the greatest Knowledge, having gained which, one can no more feel any sense of incompleteness and so none will like to add any more gains to it; having enjoyed the bliss of the Self, none will strive for a greater bliss; having known which, there will never be any thirst to know anything more. This state of absolute Bliss, Knowledge, is Brahman, the experience of the Self. This alone is the greatest gain.

All struggles to gain new acquisitions, to add fresh joys and to strive for more knowledge, indicate the sense of dissatisfaction felt by the imperfect. Imperfection belongs to the individuality in us, the ego (jīva). When the jīva rediscovers itself to be the Self, all imperfections it felt so far, are understood by it to be the destiny of its matter envelopments, the body, mind and intellect, and therefore, in that condition of spiritual rediscovery, the Realised one finds that all his struggles have ended.

That, in experiencing which, we come to feel such an endless fullness in our lives, is the supreme goal.

Verse 55

यद्दृष्ट्वा नापरं दृश्यं यद्भूत्वा न पुनर्भवः ।
यज्ज्ञात्वा नापरं ज्ञेयं तद्ब्रह्मेत्यवधारयेत् ॥ ५५ ॥

yaddṛṣṭvā nāparaṁ dṛśyaṁ yadbhūtvā na punarbhavaḥ,
yajjñātvā nāparaṁ jñeyaṁ tadbrahmetyavadhārayet. (55)

यद् दृष्ट्वा – having seen which; न – no; अपरं – other thing; दृश्यं – to be seen; यत् भूत्वा – having become which; न – not; पुनर्भवः – to be born again; यत् ज्ञात्वा – having known which; न – no; अपरं – other thing; ज्ञेयं – to be known; तत् ब्रह्म – that Brahman; इति – thus; अवधारयेत् – realise

55. *Realise that to be Brahman, having seen which nothing more remains to be seen, having become which, one is not born again in this world, and having known which, nothing remains to be known.*

In such a perfect state of tranquillity, peace and perfection, there is no further demand from within us to gain anything else to make us more perfect. If there be yet any lingering demand, then we have to consider ourselves to be still imperfect. The highest state of existence is that supreme bliss where there are no thought eruptions, when we no longer exist as the ugly ego-centre. In the experience of this absolute bliss when the mind and intellect have ceased to function, Truth dazzles forth in all its natural, divine beauty.

All intellectual endeavours are but reflections of the Self on the objects. Ātmavidyā alone gives the knowledge of the Self per se. All other (objective) knowledge of things is conditional and they are apprehended by that eternal light which illumines the entire world of its own projections. Having known the pure Awareness, nothing more remains to be known. Having become that eternal Being, the subject, there is no object any more, other than Itself, to be illumined. Having obtained a glimpse of that Reality, there is nothing more to be seen or understood. Having awakened to that Consciousness, all the misconceptions end. Having burnt our ignorance (avidyā), the seeds of bondage (vāsanās) get charred.

Verse 56

तिर्यगूर्ध्वमधः पूर्णं सच्चिदानन्दमद्वयम् ।
अनन्तं नित्यमेकं यत्तद्ब्रह्मेत्यवधारयेत् ॥ ५६ ॥

tiryagūrdhvamadhaḥ pūrṇaṁ saccidānandamadvayam,
anantaṁ nityamekaṁ yattadbrahmetyavadhārayet. (56)

तिर्यक् – all sides; ऊर्ध्वम् – above; अधः – below; पूर्णं – all-pervading; सच्चिदानन्दम् – which is Existence-Consciousness-Bliss absolute; अद्वयम् – non-dual; अनन्तं – infinite; नित्यम् – eternal; एकं – one; यत् – which; तत् ब्रह्म – that Brahman; इति – thus; अवधारयेत् – realise

56. *The one, eternal, non-dual, infinite which pervades all the quarters, above, below and all that which exists in between, which is of the nature of Existence-Consciousness-Bliss absolute – realise that to be Brahman.*

East and west, above and below, here, there and everywhere permeates that dynamic Reality. When I am aware of that Consciousness and live that experience, this outer world that I now perceive with my limited body-mind-intellect equipment, is no more available for me. How can I see the front, rear, top or bottom of that one homogeneous mass of Consciousness, when there is nothing other than It anywhere? I cannot say the 'front' – because the 'front' of what? A limited thing alone can have parts or sides. Thus, we experience this endlessness of infinite Bliss, which is one without a second. This world of attachment and sorrow is because of the self-dissipating extrovertedness and the delusory interests, wrongly created by our mind for the individuality in us.

All experiences are in the realm of duality. There is no experience when there is only one Reality alone. The nature of Paramātman in you is Sat-Cit-Ānanda. This experience of pure Being cannot be described, because in that case it will be limited by the feeble powers of our speech. It is that light which is eternal, right here in you and everywhere around you. Moments of perfect attunement with It are the moments of Self-realisation.

Verse 57

अतद्व्यावृत्तिरूपेण वेदान्तैर्लक्ष्यतेऽद्वयम् ।
अखण्डानन्दमेकं यत्तद्ब्रह्मेत्यवधारयेत् ॥ ५७ ॥

atadvyāvṛttirūpeṇa vedāntairlakṣyate'dvayam,
akhaṇḍānandamekaṁ yattadbrahmetyavadhārayet. (57)

अतद्व्यावृत्तिरूपेण – by the process of negation of what it is not; वेदान्तैः – by Vedānta; लक्ष्यते – indicated; अद्वयम् – non-dual; अखण्डानन्दम् – indivisible and blissful; एकं – one; यत् – which; तत् ब्रह्म – that Brahman; इति – thus; अवधारयेत् – realise

57. *Realise that to be Brahman which is non-dual, indivisible one and blissful, and which is indicated in Vedānta as the immutable substratum, realised after the negation of all tangible objects.*

In this verse, reference is made to the 'process of negation', which was explained earlier. None can directly reach the all-pervading Brahman because it is not an object of cognition but the subjective Reality that is ever illumining all our thoughts and actions. Being one without a second, It is not different from any similar or dissimilar objects. This indivisible and immutable Self, is not an impotent factor but a positive state of infinite Bliss. The Upaniṣads indicate that this Self is reached by a process of negation of what It is not and assertion of what It is – the very substratum for all the existence.

Are not our minds limited? Are not our thoughts ever unsteady due to impurities? Are not the objects of cognition ever-changing and of a perishable nature? What is it that is changeless in all this welter of change? What is the one Life Force on account of which there is the manifestation of matter? Who illumines the inert matter? Who injects matter with the vigour and vitality of life? What is it that exists behind the entire pluralistic existence? Which is the homogeneous and the all-permeating Spirit in all objects? What keeps all things in one loving embrace, like the string in a garland of pearls? That is the substratum, the basis of our own Self, which cannot be objectively pursued, but can be subjectively experienced as the pure Consciousness (Ātman).

Verse 58

अखण्डानन्दरूपस्य तस्यानन्दलवाश्रिताः ।
ब्रह्माद्यास्तारतम्येन भवन्त्यानन्दिनोऽखिलाः ॥ ५८ ॥

akhaṇḍānandarūpasya tasyānandalavāśritāḥ,
brahmādyāstāratamyena bhavantyānandino'khilāḥ. (58)

अखण्डानन्दरूपस्य – whose nature is unbroken Bliss; तस्य – His; आनन्दलवाश्रिताः – depending upon just a particle of this bliss; ब्रह्माद्याः – the Creator and other deities; तारतम्येन – in proportion; भवन्ति आनन्दिनः – become blissful; अखिलाः – all

58. *Deities like Brahmā and others*[1] *taste only a particle of the unlimited bliss of Brahman and proportionately enjoy their share of that particle.*

The Truth which is of the nature of absolute Bliss is eternal. However, the quantity of bliss actually enjoyed differs according to the capacity of the individual, be he an ordinary mortal, a meritorious and righteous man or a deva. An infinitesimal part of that infinite bliss is the lot for even Indra, the king of the gods. Brahmā – the Creator, the cosmic soul, tastes only a particle of that limitless bliss known as Brahmānanda.

[1] From the Creator (Brahmā), down to the most insignificant unicellular organism, all beings enjoy but a share of a minute particle of this infinite bliss of the absolute Brahman.

The joy of this entire pluralistic world depends upon just a miniscule particle of this Bliss Absolute, the Brahmānanda. How can poor mind and intellect measure the magnitude of this immeasurable depth of 'svarūpānanda'? Remember, this limitless joy is not actually measured here. We are only shown how the ethereal joy of even the Creator is but a negligible joy borrowed from Brahmānanda. In fact you are that absolute bliss itself. A relative picture has been drawn here to give us a wild quantitative measure of the infinite in terms of a finite yardstick.

The same method is employed in our daily transactions in the materialistic world as well. For example, in the annual meeting of a very successful business company, the managing directors may in their report suggest that they are planning to construct extensions involving a large sum of expenditure and may enumerate a dozen other items of expenditure, for the convenience and recreation of the staff, involving another large amount apart from a three months' bonus to all workers. The shareholders flabbergasted at this colossal amount involved would surely get ready to vote the suggestions down. But if the management were to wind up their reports saying that this entire amount, budgeted for spending is but a mere two percent of the total profits, all protests are withdrawn as everybody gets a clear picture of the total profit made.

This is the method that has been adopted here by Śaṅkara. If we are told that the Truth is of the nature of Bliss Absolute, an ordinary student does not get a clear quantitative concept of the Brahmānanda. No doubt there is happiness in everybody's life; there is none who lives as a sentient being without its limited share of joy. If all these moments of joy were to be added on, the joy so experienced by all living creatures from the Creator (Brahmā) down to a blade of grass, would be the total joy (viṣayānanda) in the universe. This sum total of the joys experienced, by all sentient beings from the day of creation till today is, as it is said here, but an infinitesimal portion of the Bliss Absolute. When this is told, the student may probably get a rough and ready concept of the absolute bliss. This is the only available method by which the Teacher can give at least a vague intellectual notion of the infinite bliss, experienced by a Man of Realisation when he has transcended all the limitations of his mortal existence.

Verse 59

तद्युक्तमखिलं वस्तु व्यवहारस्तदन्वितः।
तस्मात्सर्वगतं ब्रह्म क्षीरे सर्पिरिवाखिले ॥ ५९ ॥

tadyuktamakhilaṁ vastu vyavahārastadanvitaḥ,
tasmātsarvagataṁ brahma kṣīre sarpirivākhile. (59)

तद्युक्तम् – pervaded by that (Brahman); अखिलं – all; वस्तु – object; व्यवहारः – actions; तदन्वितः – are possible because of That; तस्मात् – therefore; सर्वगतं – all permeating; ब्रह्म – Brahman; क्षीरे – in the milk; सर्पिः – butter; इव – like; अखिले – in everything

59. *All objects are pervaded by Brahman. Also, all actions are possible because of Brahman alone. Therefore, Brahman permeates everything as butter permeates milk.*

What is real in the phenomenal world is Brahman, the substratum, and when it is all-pervading in nature, how can anything escape Its touch? It is the illuminator of all actions and thoughts, whether here within the body or there without, in the world outside. Without Its grace, the sense organs in the body are mere holes on the flesh and the outer world of objects are also gross inert matter without any symptom of life. But for this all-permeating, life-giving, fire of existence that flows through them, they all would be insentient, lifeless.

Butter permeates milk, although it is not easy for us to see it directly in the milk. Likewise Brahman permeates all objects. Butter is extracted from milk by churning. So also, the Ātman can be separated from the world of names and forms by intense meditation. And when the Spirit is experienced, there is no world of plurality any more.

Verse 60

अनण्वस्थूलमह्रस्वमदीर्घमजमव्ययम् ।
अरूपगुणवर्णाख्यं तद्ब्रह्मेत्यवधारयेत् ॥ ६० ॥

anaṇvasthūlamahrasvamadīrghamajamavyayam,
arūpaguṇavarṇākhyaṁ tadbrahmetyavadhārayet. (60)

अनणु – neither subtle; अस्थूलम् – nor gross; अह्रस्वम् – neither short; अदीर्घम् – nor long; अजम् – without birth; अव्ययम् – without change; अरूपगुणवर्णाख्यं – without form, attributes, colour and name; तत् ब्रह्म – that Brahman; इति – thus; अवधारयेत् – realise

60. *Realise that to be Brahman which is neither subtle nor gross, neither short nor long, without birth or change, without form, attributes, colour and name.*

In the last verse it was stated that all objects are pervaded by Brahman. Elaborating the point further, in this verse Brahman is referred to as neither gross nor subtle. It pervades all. It is the substratum for everything. Split or cleave even an atom and there too we find but Its presence.

Unlike finite objects which are bound by limitations of space and time and are either gross or subtle, this timeless time and spaceless space, the infinitude of the infinite cannot be bound by space, time, causation and hence, can only be defined in negative terms such as 'neither gross nor subtle'.

What is born is the body, mind and intellect and the objects of the outer world; not the Brahman who is Existence in the very progenitor of all creation, the very Knower of the first uncaused cause. This infinite Reality is irreducible, formless, attributeless with neither caste nor name. Naturally, It is indescribable. It cannot be an object of our perception, feelings or thoughts. This is the description of the Infinite in the language of negation.

Language has its own limitations. It can describe only themes that have quality (guṇa) or function (kriyā) or name (nāma) or qualification (viśeṣa) or relationship with others (sambandha). None of these are applicable for the one eternal infinite substratum for everything and hence It must elude language and remain indescribable. This technique, of describing the Infinite by the process of negation, is made use of only in the scriptures. These terms are to be considered as so many arrow marks indicating Truth; in themselves they are not positive definitions of Truth.

Verse 61

यद्भासा भास्यतेऽर्कादि भास्यैर्यत्तु न भास्यते ।
येन सर्वमिदं भाति तद्ब्रह्मेत्यवधारयेत् ॥ ६१ ॥

yadbhāsā bhāsyate'rkādi bhāsyairyattu na bhāsyate,
yena sarvamidaṁ bhāti tadbrahmetyavadhārayet. (61)

यद्भासा – by the light of which; भास्यते – are illuminated; अर्कादि – sun and others; भास्यैः – by the luminous orbs; यः – that; तु – indeed; न – not; भास्यते – is illuminated; येन – by which; सर्वम् – all; इदं – this, भाति – shines, तत् ब्रह्म – that Brahman, इति – thus, अवधारयेत् – realise

61. *That by the light of which, the luminous orbs like the sun and the moon are illuminated, but that which is not illumined by their light – realise that to be Brahman.*

The Consciousness within me illumines the world around me. The total cosmic Consciousness is the very same illuminating factor within me but without the conditionings of the individual ego. Even though the sun illumines the different worlds of creation, it also derives its life from that supreme force which is all-pervading. So, the sun and the moon do not have any special agency, other than the Self, for their illumination. That which illumines all others, which cannot be illumined by anything other than Itself is ever the illuminator and so, when there is no object for It to illumine, It illumines Itself. This Brahman, the light of Consciousness in Its own glory, is unattached and unaffected like the street lamp, an example referred to in the earlier verse. Brahman is thus the Light of all lights, the fountainhead of pure Consciousness and the mighty Illuminator of all illuminations.

Verse 62

स्वयमन्तर्बहिर्व्याप्य भासयन्नखिलं जगत्।
ब्रह्म प्रकाशते वह्निप्रतप्तायसपिण्डवत्॥ ६२॥

svayamantarbahirvyāpya bhāsayannakhilaṁ jagat,
brahma prakāśate vahnipratаptāyasapiṇḍavat. (62)

स्वयम् – Itself; अन्तः – inside; बहिः – outside; व्याप्य – pervading; भासयन् – illumining; अखिलम् – entire; जगत् – universe; ब्रह्म – Brahman; प्रकाशते – shines; वह्निप्रतप्तायसपिण्डवत् – like the fire permeating a red-hot iron ball

62. *Pervading the entire universe within and without, the supreme Brahman shines by Itself like the fire that permeates a red-hot iron ball and glows by itself.*

The supreme Brahman is the transcendental Truth which shines by Itself and It penetrates the entire world of creation. It is not something other than the world of creation, for, It exists in and through the creation all at once, as the material and the efficient cause, the pure Consciousness. Thus it is stated that the outer world of finite experience is not something different from the subjective state of Reality.

Matter without Spirit is dead, but matter and Spirit when together in their nuptial, come to express themselves in the manifestations of life. The Supreme is the vital content in every particle of this world and just as in the process of extracting butter from milk, the Spirit can be separated from matter and realised through meditation in one's own pure heart-cave.

An iron ball which has been in contact with fire for a long time comes to glow as fire itself. Similarly, even though the world of dead matter is inert, lifeless and stationary, when it plays in the vitality of the supreme Brahman, there is the manifestation of life. If the Paramātman does not lend His grace to the created objects, there is no existence for our cognition and experience. The Infinite is unborn, deathless, omnipotent and all-pervading. The created world of the things and beings is born, mortal, limited in its powers and scope. Thus, the finite and the Infinite are of opposite nature. How then can we see the intelligence and existence, which are the nature of the Self, in matter which has neither of these qualities. The red-hot iron ball example explains it.

Iron ball is black in colour and cold to the touch; fire is golden in colour and hot. The colour and the heat of fire penetrate the iron ball when it comes in contact with the fire for a sufficiently long time. So too, when inert and insentient matter is presided over by the Spirit, the Sat-Cit-Ānanda nature of the Spirit gets transferred on to the matter.

Verse 63

जगद्विलक्षणं ब्रह्म ब्रह्मणोऽन्यन्न किञ्चन ।
ब्रह्मान्यद्भाति चेन्मिथ्या यथा मरुमरीचिका ॥ ६३ ॥

jagadvilakṣaṇaṁ brahma brahmaṇo'nyanna kiñcana,
brahmānyadbhāti cenmithyā yathā marumarīcikā. (63)

जगद्विलक्षणं – which is other than the universe; **ब्रह्म** – Brahman; **ब्रह्मणः अन्यत्** – other than Brahman; **न** – not; **किञ्चन** – a little; **ब्रह्मान्यत्** – other than Brahman; **भाति** – shines; **चेत्** – if; **मिथ्या** – unreal; **यथा** – just as; **मरुमरीचिका** – the mirage

63. *Brahman is other than the universe. There exists nothing whatsoever that is not Brahman. If any object other than Brahman appears to exist, it is unreal like the mirage.*

In previous example, it was shown that the iron ball is other than the fire but glows as fire. Similarly, is the universe, which has an independent empirical existence, other than Brahman, or is it one with Brahman?

What appears as the world of diversity with its different names and forms to the ignorant is realised by the illumined to be an indivisible and non-dual Brahman. This multiplicity being illusory does not defile Brahman. In the example of desert and mirage, the desert alone exists. The ignorant sees the delusion of water pools in the desert, known as the mirage. Once a deluded mind has seen a mirage, it can multiply its misapprehension and see the waters of the mirage having waves and even the sun reflecting on the water surface and so on.

The mirage is different from the desert, yet without the desert, mirage cannot exist. And the mirage waters can never wet even a grain of the desert sand. Similarly, if one thinks that this world of plurality is real, he is mistaken, for it does not and cannot exist without Brahman. The existence of the world of plurality is like the mirage which is unreal; it can never defile the Infinite.

When the illusion, which gives us the wrong notion that the names and forms are real, ends, the perception of the plurality and the agitations caused by them in our bosom, also end. The ultimate Reality, the supreme Brahman, is different from the plurality and from that point of view It is other than the universe. Yet, from the highest standpoint, Brahman permeates the entire creation so thoroughly that there is nothing other than Brahman. Therefore, if we perceive anything different from Brahman, it can only be an unreal appearance, just like the mirage seen in the desert.

Verse 64

दृश्यते श्रूयते यद्यद्ब्रह्मणोऽन्यन्न तद्भवेत्।
तत्त्वज्ञानाच्च तद्ब्रह्म सच्चिदानन्दमद्वयम्॥ ६४ ॥

dṛśyate śrūyate yadyadbrahmaṇo'nyanna tadbhavet,
tattvajñānācca tadbrahma saccidānandamadvayam. (64)

दृश्यते – which is perceived; श्रूयते – which is heard; यत् यत् – all that; ब्रह्मणः अन्यत् – apart from Brahman; न – not; तत् – that; भवेत् – can be; तत्त्वज्ञानात् – from the knowledge of the Reality; च – and; तत् ब्रह्म – that Brahman; सच्चिदानन्दम् – which is Existence-Consciousness-Bliss absolute; अद्वयम् – non-dual

64. *All that is perceived or heard is Brahman and nothing else. Gaining the knowledge of the Reality one sees the universe as the non-dual Brahman, which is Existence-Consciousness-Bliss absolute.*

Whatever you hear, see or perceive through the sense organs cannot be anything other than the Brahman, just as whatever one sees in one's dream cannot be anything other than one's own waking state mind. The Consciousness is that which presides over and lends life to all our activities of perception, feeling and thinking. It is the Awareness in us that illumines the knowledge, ignorance, anger, love and such other hosts of feelings and emotions in us. If Consciousness does not give life to the 'prāṇa' in us, we wouldn't be alive.

Realise, therefore, that whatever exists either in this limited body, mind and intellect (microcosm) or in the outer created world (macrocosm), they are all nothing but the manifestation of Brahman alone. When this Truth is completely realised and experienced, one cannot but see the entire universe as a huge play-field in which the Paramātman alone revels as Sat-Cit-Ānanda absolute. For, He is one and one only – 'ekaṁ eva advitīyaṁ Brahma'.

Verse 65

सर्वगं सच्चिदात्मानं ज्ञानचक्षुर्निरीक्षते ।
अज्ञानचक्षुर्नेक्षेत भास्वन्तं भानुमन्धवत् ॥ ६५ ॥

sarvagaṁ saccidātmānaṁ jñānacakṣurnirīkṣate,
ajñānacakṣurnekṣeta bhāsvantaṁ bhānumandhavat. (65)

सर्वगं – which is present everywhere; सच्चिदात्मानं – Ātman which is pure Existence and Consciousness; ज्ञानचक्षुः – eye of wisdom; निरीक्षते – perceives; अज्ञानचक्षुः – one whose vision is obscured by ignorance; न – not; ईक्षेत – sees; भास्वन्तं – which is shining; भानुम् – the sun; अन्धवत् – like a blind man

65. *Though Ātman is of the nature of pure Consciousness and ever-present everywhere, yet It can only be perceived by the eye of wisdom, just as the blind do not see the resplendent sun, so too, one whose vision is obscured by ignorance does not see the Self.*

Just as a blind man cannot see the sun, so also, the person who has not developed the eye of wisdom, as his faculty of perception, is not sharpened enough to grasp the Truth; who is not discriminative enough to reject the unreal from the real; whose mind is not pure; who does not have the serene light of Knowledge within him to illumine his judgement of things; who has not done sufficient penance to acquire single pointed devotion; who still superimposes the finite qualities of the outer world of objects on the infinite Self – such an unprepared man cannot readily experience the eternal Self as his own true nature. It is not that the Ātman is not supreme, but it is the limiting factors in the seekers of Truth that veil and distort the beauty of the absolute Reality; it is the blindness of the person that makes the sun dark to him, even though the sun shines ever bright and brilliant.

All great philosophers had to, in the final analysis, take recourse to an imaginary power in the human intellect and with the help of that faculty, they explain to the intellectual students, how seekers gain the experience of the Reality. Theoretically, the Teachers of Vedānta boldly propound that on transcending all the equipments, all seekers will realise the Self, the Truth. In the beginning, the students try to follow the Teacher only with their intellect. Perception or apprehension as understood by the intellect, cannot take place without some instrument of knowing other than the object of knowledge. Carrying this impression, the student asks as to how one can experience the Truth once the body-mind-intellect equipment is transcended. For the benefit of such students the ṛṣis talk about the idea of the faculty of intuition (jñāna-cakṣu).

Through contemplative power alone can one apprehend the Reality; this apprehension is not an objective experience, it is an uncompromising and total 'becoming'.

An ordinary mind turned outward, in perceiving, feeling and thinking of the objects of the world, gets so agitated that it is rendered incapable of capturing the Supreme in its experience. The mind that is slowly and intelligently withdrawn from its extrovert fascinations and trained to turn inward, develops in itself the power to apprehend the Reality. Therefore, the intuitive power (jñāna-cakṣu) is nothing other than a mind turned inward and held in attention. In *Gītā*, a mind so prepared to act as a true vehicle to reach Knowledge, is itself known as jñānam. In this context, the twenty values of life[1] mentioned in the *Gītā*, in preparing this jñānam, are worthy of our attention.

[1] *Holy Gītā*-13.7 to 11. Humility, unpretentiousness, non-injury, forbearance, uprightness, following the Teacher, purity, steadiness, self-control, detachment from sense objects, absence of ego, constant reflection upon life's imperfections, non-attachment, non-identification with son, wife, home and the rest, constant equanimity both in conducive and non-conducive circumstances, unswerving devotion to the Lord, solitude, distaste for blabbering crowds, constant study of scriptures, and diligent attempt to understand the deeper meaning of the Reality as indicated in the scriptures. These constitute the twenty values of life.

Verse 66

श्रवणादिभिरुद्दीप्तज्ञानाग्निपरितापितः ।
जीवः सर्वमलान्मुक्तः स्वर्णवद्द्योतते स्वयम् ॥ ६६ ॥

śravaṇādibhiruddīptajñānāgniparitāpitaḥ,
jīvaḥ sarvamalānmuktaḥ svarṇavadddyotate svayam. (66)

श्रवणादिभिः – by listening and so on; उद्दीप्त – kindled; ज्ञानाग्निपरितापितः – heated in the fire of Knowledge; जीवः – the individuality; सर्वमलात् – from all impurities; मुक्तः – freed; स्वर्णवत् – like gold; द्योतते – shines; स्वयम् – by itself

66. *The jīva, on being heated in the fire of Knowledge kindled by listening to the scriptures and so on, becomes free from all impurities and shines by itself like gold.*

To gain the knowledge of Vedānta three courses are recommended – (1) listening to the Truth from the scriptures as explained by the Teacher (śravaṇa); (2) reasoning of the Truth heard (manana) and (3) deep contemplation on what has been heard and reasoned out (nididhyāsana).

Spiritual discipline is intended to cleanse the mind of its impurities. After that, removal of the ignorance (avidyā) alone enables the revelation of the absolute Truth. It is a spontaneous experience of one's own Self and an earnest seeker of Truth, who is able to kindle the fire of Knowledge in his pure heart and who is free from doubts and fears, realises the Self in him. So, the egocentric personality (jīvātman) has to rid itself of its own limitations when it rediscovers its real nature as the eternal Self. The gold ore, as it comes out of the mines is contaminated with a lot of impurities but when it is washed, heated and poured then the molten brilliance (gold) comes to acquire its real glory and beauty. So too, when the individuality is heated and purified in meditation, the Self comes to shine in its essential immortal nature.

Verse 67

हृदाकाशोदितो ह्यात्मा बोधभानुस्तमोऽपहृत्।
सर्वव्यापी सर्वधारी भाति भासयतेऽखिलम्॥ ६७॥

hṛdākāśodito hyātmā bodhabhānustamo'pahṛt,
sarvavyāpī sarvadhārī bhāti bhāsayate'khilam. (67)

हृदाकाशोदितः – which rises in the heart space; हि – verily; आत्मा – the Ātman; बोधभानुः – the sun of Knowledge; तमोऽपहृत् – destroyer of darkness; सर्वव्यापी – which pervades everything; सर्वधारी – sustains all; भाति – shines; भासयते अखिलम् – makes everything shine

67. *The Ātman, the sun of Knowledge that rises in the heart space, destroys the darkness of ignorance, pervades and sustains all, shines by Itself and also makes everything shine.*

'Hṛdaya' is generally translated as the heart. Here the term does not mean the biological organ that pumps the blood but it means the arena in the mental field from where the noble and the humane thoughts gurgle up and flow. Here, the term 'heart' is used in the same sense in which we call a man of love and goodness as a man of heart.

In that heart alone – where there is ethical purity and moral goodness – can spiritual unfoldment take place, culminating in the consequent Experience Divine.

Just as, at the approach of dawn, the darkness rolls off and light brings everything clearly to our cognition, so too, at the dawn of Wisdom, all knowledge bursts up to our awareness.

Verse 68

दिग्देशकालाद्यनपेक्ष्य सर्वगं
शीतादिहृन्नित्यसुखं निरञ्जनम् ।
यस्स्वात्मतीर्थं भजते विनिष्क्रियः
स सर्ववित्सर्वगतोऽमृतो भवेत् ॥ ६८ ॥

digdeśakālādyanapekṣya sarvagaṁ
śītādihṛnnityasukhaṁ nirañjanam,
yassvātmatīrthaṁ bhajate viniṣkriyaḥ
sa sarvavitsarvagato'mṛto bhavet. (68)

दिग्देशकालाद्यनपेक्ष्य – not depending upon direction, space and time; सर्वगं – present everywhere; शीतादिहृत् – destroys cold and so on; नित्यसुखम् – eternal Bliss; निरञ्जनम् – stainless; यः – who; स्वात्मतीर्थम् – the holy place of his own Ātman; भजते – worships; विनिष्क्रियः – renouncing all activities; सः – He; सर्ववित् – all knowing; सर्वगतः – all-pervading; अमृतः – immortal; भवेत् – becomes

68. *One who renounces all activities, who is free of all the limitations of direction, space and time, who worships his own Ātman – which is present everywhere, which is the destroyer of heat and cold, which is stainless and eternal Bliss – becomes all knowing and all-pervading, and thereafter, attains immortality.*

Whether the sea is stormy or calm, the sun always shines on it. Similarly, the pure Ātman – the Truth which is beyond time, space and causality, which is all-pervading, which has no duality, which is the pure Consciousness in all awareness, which is the substratum on which all the pluralistic things play about – is the one Consciousness which illumines the entire creation. Without It, nothing will ever exist anywhere. Know that to be your own Self.

The Mahātman who renounces all his desires, activities, attachments, likes and dislikes and his very contact with the life in this ephemeral world of objects, who is ever at the shrine of the Ātman striving with determination to experience the bliss of his own Self, becomes all knowing, all-pervasive Brahman Itself. Having experienced that which has no beginning or end, he becomes immortal. The dreamer, when he ends his dreams and wakes up, becomes the waker himself; the limited ego on transcending the mind-intellect equipment itself becomes the immortal Brahman.

OM TAT SAT